DEATH WITHOUT DIGNITY

DEATH WITHOUT DIGNITY:

Euthanasia in Perspective

edited by
Nigel M. de S. Cameron

with a foreword by
Bishop Maurice A.P. Wood

RUTHERFORD HOUSE BOOKS
Edinburgh

Published by Rutherford House, 17 Claremont Park,
Edinburgh EH6 7PJ, Scotland

ISBN 0 946068 42 9

Copyright ©1990 Rutherford House and Contributors

Computer typeset at Rutherford House on Apple Macintosh™
Printed in Great Britain by Billing & Sons Ltd, Worcester

————Contents————

———Foreword———

The Rt Revd Maurice Wood DSC MA RNR

Most of these important papers were delivered at the crowded 'Death with Dignity?' conference in the Queen Elizabeth II Conference Centre in March 1989. They are more timely than ever, now that the Embryology Bill is before Parliament and the nation.

Dr Cameron's biblical perspective theologically complemented Luke Gormally's philosophical approach, and opened our minds to consider the sharp ethical problems posed by Dr Anthony Smith, over against his background of missionary leadership, and his insight from St Christopher's Hospice.

The morning lectures demonstrate that calm opposition to the threat of euthanasia is based on strong Christian, biblical and ethical foundations, and not just on emotion. We were privileged in the afternoon to hear wisdom based on long practical experience, with true Christian caring, from Dr Cicely Saunders, and I was reminded that a strong supporter of euthanasia once told me that only the hospice movement, under-girded by the religious stress on the sanctity of life, could withstand the demands of euthanasia.

Dr Robert George and Miss Sarah Whitfield helped us to see that strong Christian teaching in the practical world of patient care, even in the AIDS situation, could overcome the apparent dichotomy between a 'kindly' view of euthanasia practice, over against a 'firm' view of biblical doctrine.

Compassion, supported by selfless and honest caring for dying patients, and especially when supported by loving Christian medical and nursing treatment, is on the side of hospice philosophy, rather than euthanasia theory.

The grim spectre of the breakdown of total trust, between dying patients and euthanasia-orientated doctors, was brought before us by the accounts of the Dutch experience.

Although, as these papers show, we were not arguing from dogmatic religious positions, time and again, both implicitly and explicitly, the strong Christian and also Jewish insights came through. 'So God created man in his own image, in the image of God, he created him: male and female he created them' (Genesis 2:27).

For my part as a Christian believer, and taking part in the conference as Chairman of the Order of Christian Unity, I was glad openly to affirm my belief in the sanctity of human life, and its God-given uniqueness in the animal kingdom. Basically I believe that the coming of Jesus the Son of God to our world, as one of us, raises humanity to a level which calls not only believing Christians, but all with such moral principle, to guard the miracle of human life from the moment of conception, and also to protect the dying, that they may go to their Maker with dignity, without fear, and with all medical and pain-relieving treatments now available, and – as we try to do in the hospice movement – 'never alone'.

Without undue pressure, and with humble Christian witness and caring, many sick people are now finding eternal life through faith in Christ Jesus, as their earthly life is ebbing away. That is a base line worth all the toil and compassionate caring, which breathes through this compilation of papers from a great conference.

Bishop Maurice Wood
Chairman, Order of Christian Unity

—————Introduction—————

Although the word 'euthanasia' literally means a good or easy death, it has long been associated with what is better and more simply called 'mercy-killing'. The assumption, of course, is that in many circumstances the only route to good or easy death is that offered by 'euthanasia', a 'death with dignity' - as the euphemistic euthanasia slogan has it. Since many people fear death, and are especially fearful of dying slowly and in pain, there is wide popular support for the idea. It has been less popular in two important quarters: among doctors (a recent British Medical Association report re-iterated opposition to the idea), and among legislators (attempts to introduce euthanasia bills into Parliament have all flopped). The medical profession is of course better informed than the public of the remarkable resources at their disposal to control pain and discomfort in chronic and terminal sickness, and most doctors well understand that allowing a patient to die in peace when the dying process is already well advanced and irreversible has always been considered good medical practice. There can be no doubt that opinion poll support for voluntary euthanasia depends decisively on general misunderstanding and needless fear in this matter. For their part, peers and MPs better understand the ethical and legal complexity of permitting an exception to the fundamental idea that killing people is wrong, whatever the motive. This is not the place to rehearse the arguments which are laid out at some length in the chapters which follow, but we may ask the single question why in our medical tradition there should have been such wholehearted repudiation of euthanasia. Even one generation back we were much less able to cope with the control of pain and distress in terminal care. In ancient times, when the Hippocratic physicians who were the founders of modern medicine set their face against taking life as an option in clinical management, the alternatives were drastically limited. Yet their conviction that medicine was about healing was so firm that it remains the cornerstone of mainstream medical thinking today. The recent development of the hospice movement and increasing focus on palliative medicine - where cure is not possible - bears eloquent testimony to the continuing power of Hippocratism, even in the face of much ethical uncertainty in the medical profession as in society as a whole.

Euthanasia is better called mercy-killing, since that is what it is: killing out of a motive which is claimed to be that of mercy. The current debate is focused on the demand for *voluntary* euthanasia - mercy-killing at the request of the patient. Sometimes this is compared to 'assisted suicide', as if it were a simple extension of the freedom to take one's own life. If it is truly voluntary then plainly the desire for self-destruction is common to suicide and voluntary euthanasia. But even voluntary mercy-killing remains an act of killing. And leaving aside the ethics of suicide, the problem remains of determining whether truly voluntary choices are possible in so profound a decision. What of the direct and indirect influence of relatives, who may stand to gain much? What of the lead given by the doctor - and by the very fact that the medical profession approves the practice? What of the patient exhibiting symptoms of clinical depression, which is often the context for a request to a doctor to intervene? And what of the incompetent patient? May relatives truly take up the torch of patient autonomy when their interests can conflict with those of the patient in subtle and complex ways? A rigorous examination of the character of this act of 'volunteering' is plainly central to an understanding of this defence of mercy-killing.

Yet that raises the question that lies behind the debate about voluntary euthanasia, that of *in*voluntary euthanasia: mercy-killing at the choice of others. It is arguable that the logic of euthanasia depends finally upon the concept of a life that is not worth living: how, for example, do we decide whether a request for euthanasia is reasonable or not, save by reference to some such concept? Yet once such a concept is recognised, we have criteria by which those who are held to be incompetent may be subjected to euthanasia involuntarily; and it becomes *un*reasonable for certain classes of competent patient to fail to volunteer. The voluntary-involuntary distinction is recognised by supporters of euthanasia as vital in their campaign for euthanasia to be legalised; but it is much less plain than they suggest.

A series of other questions immediately demands discussion: the distinction between 'active' and 'passive' euthanasia (which if the doctor's motive is the same - to bring about the patient's death when the dying process is neither advanced nor irreversible - is a distinction without much of a difference); the problem of advance directives and the 'living will' (an increasingly popular way of requesting passive euthanasia in advance, which raises grave ethical and practical problems); the significance of two major developments in the 1980's - the wide incidence of mercy-killing by doctors in Holland, and the spread of HIV and AIDS; and, behind all this, the question of the meaning of human life which will offer a context for the significance of human suffering and death. All these are raised, and some discussed at length, in the chapters which follow.

The greater part of these papers originated at a conference co-sponsored by the Christian Medical Fellowship, CARE, the Order of Christian Unity and Rutherford House at the Queen Elizabeth II Conference Centre in Westminster during the spring of 1989. Several others (Cook, Higginson, Vere) were read during a conference convened earlier by Christian Impact at the Institute for Contemporary Christianity. The remainder reprint articles which need to be widely available as this debate continues to run its course (Alexander, Koop). These chapters bring together clinicians, philosophers and theologians in the kind of inter-disciplinary debate which is becoming increasingly common as the context for bioethical discussion. We trust that they will be read and provide doctors, nurses, ministers, students and others with resource material on what is sure to be among the major talking-points of the 1990's.

Nigel M de S. Cameron
Rutherford House, Edinburgh
January 1990

An International Perspective: Deliberate Death in Holland

Karel Gunning

I have been asked to speak to you today on euthanasia in Holland. I would like to begin by saying that I love my country very much, and that I am proud of many of its achievements in the past, but that I am deeply ashamed of what is happening in Holland just now. I would also like to mention the fact that during the last war Dutch doctors refused to cooperate with the German euthanasia programme, thereby risking imprisonment and deportation. And I well remember that forty years ago, when I was a medical student, we learned that if a doctor deliberately killed a patient he would be jailed - and would lose his medical licence for ever. So you can see that there have been times when we Dutch have been very much opposed to euthanasia.

But during the last fifteen years our courts have almost ceased to prosecute doctors who commit euthanasia providing they stick to certain rules. The result is that our Inspector General of Health estimated some time ago that the number of cases of euthanasia is at around 10,000 a year - that is somewhere between the highest estimate of 18,000 a year and the lowest of 6,000. As the total number of deaths in our country is only 120,000 a year, this means that between 5% and 15% of our annual deaths are the result of deliberate killing by doctors. Of course we have to rely on estimates, as most cases of euthanasia are not reported. Only in around 140 cases a year does the doctor inform the police that he has committed euthanasia - one in 40 if the lowest estimate is right, and one in 100 if the highest. We must add that the number of patients who *ask* for death is estimated at 2,000 a year, which means that at least 4,000 and possibly 16,000 patients a year have their lives ended without their consent.

I have given you some cold figures. May I repeat some of them again in order to help us better realize what is happening. Our senior health inspector estimates the number of patients who are deliberately put to death at 10,000 a year. Ten thousand! And Holland continues to live as if nothing extraordinary is taking place. We worry about South Africa, we worry about seals and acid rain, and I agree that we need to find solutions for these problems. But is it a normal thing to accept that 10,000 patients a year are put to death? And what are we to think of our government, which believes that the solution is to change the law so that doctors who commit euthanasia would notify the police without fear of being punished? The government is not worried about the killing as such, but that most of these killings go unreported.

Now the debate is about euthanasia, but I like to avoid this term because it can be given so many meanings. The ancient Greeks used 'euthanasia' to say that someone had died a good and easy death. And of course we all wish a good death for ourselves, and for anybody else. But in the actual debate the term is used *not* for dying a good death, but for a kind of killing which is supposed to be good. The bill which our government has introduced and which will soon be debated in the Dutch parliament defines euthanasia as 'deliberate killing of a patient at his own request'. The result of the euthanasia debate has been that we have been brainwashed into believing that ending a patient's life at his own request is quite different from ending his life at the request of someone else. We have been made to believe that killing a patient at his own request is good - and that not killing him is bad. Simply by the use of the term 'euthanasia', to mean 'good killing', the battle to get the deliberate ending of someone's life accepted as a good thing has been won from the very beginning. In order to clear our thinking, I believe we should drop the ambiguous term 'euthanasia', and speak instead of deliberate killing, for that is actually what we are debating about.

Instead of asking whether euthanasia is good, we should ask ourselves whether deliberate killing can ever be. Many Dutch people are afraid of pain. That is quite understandable, because the way we treat pain is often quite insufficient. In Holland we are only now starting to develop the kind of hospice care which you in Britain have already pioneered. Two years ago a Dutch government committee reported that too many doctors in Holland were unfamiliar with the newest methods to treat pain. A survey had shown that in 53% of cases of cancer with pain, the patient was suffering unnecessarily - that is, there was pain which could have been taken away if the doctor had known how. No wonder that patients ask doctors to put an end to their suffering! But instead of ending the patient's life, doctors in Holland should learn to treat pain the way you do in Britain. Our conclusion must be that in these cases deliberate killing is certainly not a good thing.

But pain is not the only reason for a patient to ask for death. Some people are lonely. Some people fear that they are losing their attractiveness and may become so repellent that their relatives and friends will cease to visit them. I don't think I have to tell you what we can do for these patients, as your hospices have already shown the answer. In these hospices patients find new friends: the other patients, the doctors, the nurses who visit them in their homes, *etc.* By the way the patient is treated he feels that, though the exterior may have changed, his inner self has lost nothing of its value. By contrast the doctor admits that in these circumstances ending the patient's life would be the best solution; this actually confirms the patient's worst fears. His life *has* lost its value, indeed he is too repellent to live. Again, our conclusion must be that in these cases too deliberate killing is certainly not good.

But going from case to case is not the way to answer the question whether deliberate killing can ever be good. We should ask in the first place whether human life is sacred. For if it is, then deliberate killing can never be good. The problem with the term 'sanctity of life', however, is that it has a religious connotation which I would like to avoid. It is true that most religions forbid deliberate killing, but I think we must produce an answer to our question which is valid and acceptable for every human being, irrespective of his religion. Therefore I prefer the term 'inviolability of life', which has exactly the same meaning as sanctity, but does not give the impression of having a religious origin.

Is human life inviolable? 'Yes' is the answer of the Universal Declaration of Human Rights, which says in Article 3: 'Everyone has the right to life, liberty and security of person.' 'Yes' is the answer of the European Convention for the Protection of Human Rights and Fundamental Freedoms, which in Article 2 proclaims:

'Everyone's right to life shall be protected by law.' 'Yes' say our governments, when they unite in their effort to put an end to terrorism, *etc.* And when we read about the millions of refugees in all parts of the world, people who have left their country because they fear being killed there, we come to the conclusion that all these people want to live in a country where their lives are protected by law - and where the law is obeyed.

In fact the question is not whether human life *is* inviolable, but whether we *want* it to be inviolable. If we want our lives to be protected by the law, then we must decide that human life is inviolable, which means that each human life is inviolable and that it is never permissible to end the life of a human being. Then, even if we are obliged to kill in order to save the lives of others, this killing is not allowed, it is not called good, but we speak of *force majeure*, which means that the person who has killed is punishable but may be exculpated. Either human life is inviolable, or it is destructible. We can't have it both ways. If we make one exception, where deliberate killing is called good in order to solve a problem, then human life is no longer inviolable but has become destructible instead. If we decide that human life is inviolable, then everybody's life must be protected by law. Then also my own life is protected by law, and I am not allowed to kill myself or ask someone else to kill me. If we want our lives to be protected, that is the price we have to pay.

Until now deliberate killing has been regarded as something abhorrent in Western society. If we begin to accept killing as a good thing in order to solve one kind of problem, then we will soon find reasons to use killing in order to solve other kinds of problems. And history provides many examples of the kind of society we get, if killing is regarded as good. We must decide what kind of society we really want for ourselves and for future generations.

Having decided for ourselves whether human life should be inviolable or destructible, we can now study the Dutch situation, which today focuses around the government's bill. The title of the bill is impressive: 'Rules concerning the careful medical conduct of a doctor who appeals to *force majeure* when ending the life of a patient at his explicit and earnest request'. This title itself raises already a number of questions, most of which are better dealt with when discussing the text of the bill. I would like simply to point out the government's apparent intention to regard ending a patient's life *as a medical act*, disregarding the fact that medical practice through the ages has always excluded deliberate killing.

The text of the bill consists of two parts. The first part reconfirms the existing law, which explicitly forbids killing a person at his own request. The second part is an addition to the present law concerning medical practice. It states first what is *not* considered to be euthanasia, such as refraining from life-saving treatment at the patient's own request, and causing death as a side-effect of combatting pain. Secondly it gives a set of rules which the doctor should apply if he wants to claim *force majeure*. The doctor must ascertain that the patient's request to die is geniune, lasting, and made without any pressure from other people. The doctor must explain to the patient his present state of health, the prognosis and the possibilities of dealing with the disease and its symptoms. The doctor must consult a colleague and also, if the patient allows it, the family. And the doctor must inform the police and keep a record of all the pertinent facts, which must be kept for a period of five years and made available to the court if requested.

You will see that the bill is very cleverly conceived. Euthanasia remains a crime, and the doctor is not allowed to kill his patient. Even if he obeys the rules he cannot be sure that he will not be punished. Thus the government hopes to convince its European partners that our country does not trespass against Article 2 of the European Convention, which says that everyone's life must be protected by the law. The bill does not legalize euthanasia, but it gives the doctor the opportunity to kill a patient without being punished - by claiming *force majeure*. This claim is based on the idea that the doctor feels a conflict of duties. On the one hand he feels a duty to fulfil the patient's wish to die. Of course there is no real conflict of duties, as the doctor is not allowed to kill and there are better ways to help the patient without killing him; but no court will punish a doctor who has applied these rules.

Of course there are other objections. After the patient's death it is very hard to verify the doctor's statement that the patient was killed at his own request, so the door is wide open to killing a patient without or even against his own wish. Can a doctor ever be sure that the patient's request was made without any pressure from other (interested) persons? If the doctor does not know how to treat pain effectively, his prognosis will be very gloomy. But the one major objection is that human life is no longer inviolable.

If Holland succeeds in accepting this euthanasia bill, other countries will try the same procedure. I think we have to decide now whether human life should be inviolable, whether we are happy with the alternative - that it is destructible. The member-states of the European Community have taken stern measures because Iran has threatened to kill a writer who insulted Islam. I understand the feelings of Moslems, as I understand the feelings of patients who ask for death. But if we decide that human life is inviolable, then we have to protect *everyone's* life. In Holland it is not just one man's life that is threatened, but 10,000 people actually being killed each year. What is the answer of the international community to this mass killing in Holland?

2

Medical Science under Dictatorship

Leo Alexander

We are grateful to the New England Journal of Medicine *for permission to reprint this paper, first published by them in 241:2, pp 39-47 (July 1949). Dr Alexander was a psychiatrist who worked with the Office of the Chief of Counsel for War Crimes at Nuremberg between 1946 and 1947.*

Science under dictatorship becomes subordinated to the guiding philosophy of the dictatorship. Irrespective of other ideologic trappings, the guiding philosophic principle of recent dictatorships, including that of the Nazis, has been Hegelian in that what has been considered 'rational utility' and corresponding doctrine and planning has replaced moral, ethical and religious values. Nazi propaganda was highly effective in perverting public opinion and public conscience, in a remarkably short time. In the medical profession this expressed itself in a rapid decline in standards of professional ethics. Medical science in Nazi Germany collaborated with this Hegelian trend particularly in the following enterprises: the mass extermination of the chronically sick in the interest of saving 'useless' expenses to the community as a whole; the mass extermination of those considered socially disturbing or racially and ideologically unwanted; the individual, inconspicuous extermination of those considered disloyal within the ruling group; and the ruthless use of 'human experimental material' for medico-military research.

This paper discusses the origins of these activities, as well as their consequences upon the body social, and the motivation of those participating in them.

Preparatory Propaganda

Even before the Nazis took open charge in Germany, a propaganda barrage was directed against the traditional compassionate nineteenth-century attitudes toward the chronically ill, and for the adoption of a utilitarian, Hegelian point of view. Sterilization and euthanasia of persons with chronic mental illnesses was discussed at a meeting of Bavarian psychiatrists in 1931.[1]   By 1936 extermination of the physically or socially unfit was so openly accepted that its practice was mentioned incidentally in an article published in an official German medical journal.[2]

Lay opinion was not neglected in this campaign. Adults were propagandized by motion pictures, one of which, entitled 'I Accuse', deals entirely with euthanasia. This film depicts the life history of a woman suffering from multiple sclerosis; in it her husband, a doctor, finally kills her to the accompaniment of soft piano music rendered by

---

[1]   Bumke, O. Discussion of Faltlhauser K. Zur Frage der Sterilisierung geistig Abnormer. *Allg. Ztschr. f. Psychiat.* 96:372, 1932.
[2]   Dierichs, R. Beitrag zur psychischen Anstaltsbehandlung Tuberkulöser. *Ztschr. f. Tuberk.* 74:21-28, 1936.

a sympathetic colleague in an adjoining room. Acceptance of this ideology was implanted even in the children. A widely used high-school mathematics text, 'Mathematics in the Service of National Political Education'[3] , includes problems stated in distorted terms of the cost of caring for and re-habilitating the chronically sick and crippled. One of the problems asked, for instance, how many new housing units could be built and how many marriage-allowance loans could be given to newly wedded couples for the amount of money it cost the state to care for 'the crippled, the criminal and the insane'.

Euthanasia

The first direct order for euthanasia was issued by Hitler on September 1, 1939, and an organization was set up to execute the program. Dr Karl Brandt headed the medical section, and Phillip Bouhler the administrative section. All state institutions were required to report on patients who had been ill five years or more and who were unable to work, by filling out questionnaires giving name, race, marital status, nationality, next of kin, whether regularly visited and by whom, who bore financial responsibility and so forth. The decision regarding which patients should be killed was made entirely on the basis of this brief information by expert consultants, most of whom were professors of psychiatry in the key universities. These consultants never saw the patients themselves. The thoroughness of their scrutiny can be appraised by the work of one expert, who between November 14 and December 1, 1940, evalued 2109 questionnaires.

---

[3]   Dorner, A. *Mathematik in Dienste der Nationalpolitischen Erzichung: Ein handbuch für Lehrer, Herausgegeben in Auftrage des Reichsverbandes Deutscher mathematischer Gesellschaften und Vereine.* Second edition, (revised). Frankfurt: Moritz Diesterweg, 1935. Pp. 1-118. Third edition (revised), 1936. Pp. 1-118.

These questionnaires were collected by a 'Realm's Work Committee of Institutions for Cure and Care'.[4]   A parallel organization devoted exclusively to the killing of children was known by the similarly euphemistic name of 'Realm's Committee for Scientific Approach to Severe Illness Due to Heredity and Constitution'. The 'Charitable Transport Company for the Sick' transported patients to the killing centers, and the 'Charitable Foundation for Institutional Care' was in charge of collecting the cost of the killings from the relatives, without, however, informing them what the charges were for; in the death certificates the cause of death was falsified.

What these activities meant to the population at large was well expressed by a few hardy souls who dared to protest. A member of the court of appeals at Frankfurt-am-Main wrote in December 1939:

There is constant discussion of the question of the destruction of socially unfit life - in the places where there are mental institutions, in neighbouring towns, sometimes over a large area, throughout the Rhineland, for example. The people have come to recognize the vehicles in which the patients are taken from their original institution to the intermediate institution and from there to the liquidation institution. I am told that when they see these buses even the children call out: 'They're taking some more people to be gassed.'   From Limburg it is reported that every day from one to three buses with shades drawn pass through on the way from Weilmunster to Hadamar, delivering inmates to the liquidation institution there. According to the stories the arrivals are immediately stripped to the

---

4   Alexander, L. Public mental health practices in Germany, sterilization and execution of patients suffering from nervous or mental disease, Combined Intelligence Objectives Subcommittee. Item No. 24. File No. XXVIII-50. Pp. 1-173 (August), 1945.

skin, dressed in paper shirts, and forthwith taken to a gas chamber, where they are liquidated with hydrocyanic acid gas and an added anesthetic. The bodies are reported to be moved to a combustion chamber by means of a conveyor belt, six bodies to a furnace. The resulting ashes are then distributed into six urns which are shipped to the families. The heavy smoke from the crematory building is said to be visible over Hadamar every day. There is talk, furthermore, that in some cases heads and other portions of the body are removed for anatomical examination. The people working at this liquidation job in the institutions are said to be assigned from other areas and are shunned completely by the populace. This personnel is described as frequenting the bars at night and drinking heavily. Quite apart from these overt incidents that exercise the imagination of the people, they are disquieted by the question of whether old folk who have worked hard all their lives and may merely have come into their dotage are also being liquidated. There is talk that the homes for the aged are to be cleaned out too. The people are said to be waiting for legislative regulation providing some orderly method that will insure especially that the aged feeble-minded are not included in the program.

Here one sees what 'euthanasia' means in actual practice. According to the records, 275,000 people were put to death in these killing centers. Ghastly as this seems, it should be realized that this was merely the entering wedge for exterminations of far greater scope in the political program for genocide of conquered nations and the racially unwanted. The methods used and personnel trained in the killing centers for the chronically sick became the nucleus of the much larger centers in the East, where the plan was to kill all Jews and Poles and to cut down the Russian population by 30,000,000.

The original program developed by Nazi hotheads
included also the genocide of the English, with the
provision that the English males were to be used as
laborers in the vacated territories in the East, there to be
worked to death, whereas the English females were to be
brought into Germany to improve the qualities of the
German race. (This was indeed a peculiar admission on
the part of the German eugenists.)

In Germany the exterminations included the mentally
defective, psychotics (particularly schizophrenics),
epileptics and patients suffering from infirmities of old age
and from various organic neurological disorders such as
infantile paralysis, Parkinsonism, multiple sclerosis and
brain tumors. The technical arrangements, methods and
training of the killer personnel were under the direction of a
committee of physicians and other experts headed by Dr
Karl Brandt. The mass killings were first carried out with
carbon monoxide gas, but later cyanide gas ('cyclon B')
was found to be more effective. The idea of camouflaging
the gas chambers as shower baths was developed by
Brack, who testified before Judge Sebring that the patients
walked in calmly, deposited their towels and stood with
their little pieces of soap under the shower outlets, waiting
for the water to start running. This statement was ample
rebuttal of his claim that only the most severely regressed
patients among the mentally sick and only the moribund
ones among the physically sick were exterminated. In
truth, all those unable to work and considered
nonrehabilitable were killed.

All but their squeal was utilized. However, the program
grew so big that even scientists who hoped to benefit from
the treasure of material supplied by this totalitarian
method were disappointed. A neuropathologist, Dr
Hallervorden, who had obtained 500 brains from the killing

centers for the insane, gave me a vivid first-hand account.[5] The Charitable Transport Company for the Sick brought the brains in batches of 150 to 250 at a time. Hallervorden stated:

> There was wonderful material among those brains, beautiful mental defectives, malformations and early infantile diseases. I accepted those brains of course. Where they came from and how they came to me was really none of my business.

In addition to the material he wanted, all kinds of other cases were mixed in, such as patients suffering from various types of Parkinsonism, simple depressions, involutional depressions and brain tumors, and all kinds of other illnesses, including psychopathy that had been difficult to handle.

These were selected from the various wards of the institutions according to an excessively simple and quick method. Most institutions did not have enough physicians, and what physicians there were were either too busy or did not care, and they delegated the selection to the nurses and attendants. Whoever looked sick or was otherwise a problem was put on a list and was transported to the killing center. The worst thing about this business was that it produced a certain brutalization of the nursing personnel. They got to simply picking out those whom they did not like, and the doctors had so many patients that they did not even know them, and put their names on the list.

---

5   *Idem.* Neuropathology and neurophysiology, including electro-encephalography in wartime Germany. Combined Intelligence Objectives Subcommittee Item No. 24, File No. XXVII-1. Pp. 1-65 (July), 1945.

Of the patients thus killed, only the brains were sent to
Dr Hallervorden; they were killed in such large numbers
that autopsies of the bodies were not feasible. That, in Dr
Hallervorden's opinion, greatly reduced the scientific value
of the material. The brains, however, were always well
fixed and suspended in formaline, exactly according to his
instructions. He thinks that the cause of psychiatry was
permanently injured by these activities, and that
psychiatrists have lost the respect of the German people
forever. Dr Hallervorden concluded: 'Still, there were
interesting cases in this material.'

In general only previously hospitalized patients were
exterminated for reasons of illness. An exception is a
program carried out in a northwestern district of Poland,
the 'Warthegau', where a health survey of the entire
population was made by an 'SS X-Ray Battalion' headed
by Professor Hohlfelder, radiologist of the University of
Frankfurt-am-Main. Persons found to be infected with
tuberculosis were carted off to special extermination
centers.

It is rather significant that the German people were
considered by their Nazi leaders more ready to accept the
exterminations of the sick than those for political reasons.
It was for that reason that the first exterminations of the
latter group were carried out under the guise of sickness.
So-called 'psychiatric experts' were dispatched to survey
the inmates of camps with the specific order to pick out
members of racial minorities and political offenders from
occupied territories and to dispatch them to killing centers
with specially made diagnoses such as that of 'inveterate
German hater' applied to a number of prisoners who had
been active in the Czech underground.

Certain classes of patients with mental diseases who
were capable of performing labor, particularly members of
the armed forces suffering from psychopathy or neurosis,

were sent to concentration camps to be worked to death, or to be reassigned to punishment battalions and to be exterminated in the process of removal of mine fields.[6]

A large number of those marked for death for political or racial reasons were made available for 'medical' experiments involving the use of involuntary human subjects. From 1942 on, such experiments carried out in concentration camps were openly presented at medical meetings. This program included 'terminal human experiments', a term introduced by Dr Rascher to denote an experiment so designed that its successful conclusion depended upon the test person's being put to death.

The Science of Annihilation

A large part of this research was devoted to the science of destroying and preventing life, for which I have proposed the term 'ktenology', the science of killing.[7-9] In the course of the ktenologic research, methods of mass killing and mass sterilization were investigated and developed for use against non-German peoples or Germans who were considered useless.

Sterilization methods were widely investigated, but proved impractical in experiments conducted in concentration camps. A rapid method developed for sterilization of females, which could be accomplished in the

---

6   *Idem.* German military neuropsychiatry and neurosurgery. Combined Intelligence Objectives Subcommittee, Item No. 24, File No. XXVIII-49. Pp. 1-138 (August), 1945.

7-9 7.   *Idem.* Sociopsyvhologic structure of SS: pschiatric report of Nuremberg trials for war crimes. *Arch. Neurol. & Psychiat.* 59:622-634, 1948.

8.   *Idem.* War crimes: their social-psychological aspects. *Am.J. Psychiat.* 105:170-177, 1948.

9.   *Idem.* War crimes and their motivation: socio-psychological structure of SS and criminalization of society. *J.Crim. Law & Criminol.* 39:294-326, 1948.

course of a regular health examination, was the intra-uterine injection of various chemicals. Numerous mixtures were tried, some with iodopine and others containing barium; another was most likely silver nitrate with iodized oil, because the result could be ascertained by x-ray examination. The injections were extremely painful, and a number of women died in the course of the experiments. Professor Karl Clauberg reported that he had developed a method at the Auschwitz concentration camp by which he could sterilize 1000 women in one day.

Another method of sterilization, or rather castration, was proposed by Viktor Brack especially for conquered populations. His idea was that X-ray machinery could be built into desks at which the people would have to sit, ostensibly to fill out a questionnaire requiring five minutes; they would be sterilized without being aware of it. This method failed because experiments carried out on 100 male prisoners brought out the fact that severe x-ray burns were produced on all subjects. In the course of this research, which was carried out by Dr Horst Schuman, the testicles of the victims were removed for histologic examination two weeks later. I myself examined 4 castrated survivors of this ghastly experiment. Three had extensive necrosis of the skin near the genitalia, and the other an extensive necrosis of the urethra. Other experiments in sterilization used an extract of the plant *Caladium seguinum*, which had been shown in animal studies by Madaus and his co-workers[10] [11] to cause selective necrosis of the germinal cells of the testicles as well as the ovary.

[10]   Madaus, G., and Koch, F.E. Tierexperimentelle Studien zur Frage der medikamentösen Sterilisierung (durch Caladium seguinum (Dieffenbachia seguina). *Ztschr. f. d. ges. exper. Med.* 109:68-87, 1941.

[11]   Madaus. G. Zauberpflanzen im Lichte experimenteller Forschung, Das Schweigrohr - Caladium seguinum. *Umschau* 24:600-602, 1941.

The development of methods for rapid and inconspicuous individual execution was the objective of another large part of the ktenologic research. These methods were to be applied to members of the ruling group, including the SS itself, who were suspected of disloyalty. This, of course, is an essential requirement in a dictatorship, in which 'cut-throat competition' becomes a grim reality, and any hint of faintheartedness or lack of enthusiasm for the methods of totalitarian rule is considered a threat to the entire group.

Poisons were the subject of many of these experiments. A research team at the Buchenwald concentration camp, consisting of Drs Joachim Mrugowsky, Erwin Ding-Schuler and Waldemar Hoven, developed the most widely used means of individual execution under the guise of medical treatment - namely, the intravenous injection of phenol or gasoline. Several alkaloids were also investigated, among them aconitine, which was used by Dr Hoven to kill several imprisoned former fellow SS men who were potential witnesses against the camp commander, Koch, then under investigation by the SS. At the Dachau concentration camp Dr Rascher developed the standard cyanide capsules, which could be easily bitten through, either deliberately or accidentally, if mixed with certain foods, and which, ironically enough, later became the means with which Himmler and Goering killed themselves. In connection with these poison experiments there is an interesting incident of characteristic sociologic significance. When Dr Hoven was under trial by the SS the investigating SS judge, Dr Morgen, proved Dr Hoven's guilt by feeding the poison found in Dr Hoven's possession to a number of Russian prisoners of war; these men died with the same symptoms as the SS men murdered by Dr Hoven. This worthy judge was rather proud of this efficient method of proving Dr Hoven's guilt and appeared entirely unaware of the fact that in the process he had committed murder himself.

Poisons, however, proved too obvious or detectable to
be used for the elimination of high-ranking Nazi party
personnel who had come into disfavor, or of prominent
prisoners whose deaths should appear to stem from
natural causes. Phenol or gasoline, for instance, left a
telltale odor with the corpse. For this reason a number of
more subtle methods were devised. One of these was
artificial production of septicemia. An intramuscular
injection of 1 cc. of pus, containing numerous chains of
streptococci, was the first step. The site of injection was
usually the inside of the thigh, close to the adductor canal.
When an abscess formed it was tapped and 3 cc. of the
creamy pus removed was injected intravenously into the
patient's opposite arm. If the patient then died from
septicemia, the autopsy proved that death was caused by
the same organism that had caused the abscess. These
experiments were carried out in many concentration
camps. At the Dachau camp the subjects were almost
exclusively Polish Catholic priests. However, since this
method did not always cause death, sometimes resulting
merely in a local abscess, it was considered inefficient, and
research was continued with other means but along the
same lines.

The final triumph of the part of ktenologic research aimed
at finding a method of inconspicuous execution that would
produce autopsy findings indicative of death from natural
causes was the development of repeated intravenous
injections of suspensions of live tubercle bacilli, which
brought on acute miliary tuberculosis within a few weeks.
This method was produced by Professor Dr Heissmeyer,
who was one of Dr Gebhardt's associates at the SS
hospital of Hohenlychen. As a means of further
camouflage, so that the SS at large would not suspect the
purpose of these experiments, the preliminary tests for the
efficacy of this method were performed exclusively on

children imprisoned in the Neuengamme concentration camp.

For use in 'medical' executions of prisoners and of members of the SS and other branches of the German armed forces the use of simple lethal injections, particularly phenol injections, remained the instrument of choice. Whatever methods he used, the physician gradually became the unofficial executioner, for the sake of convenience, informality and relative secrecy. Even on German submarines it was the physician's duty to execute the troublemakers among the crew by lethal injections.

Medical science has for some time been an instrument of military power in that it preserved the health and fighting efficiency of troops. This essentially defensive purpose is not inconsistent with the ethical principles of medicine. In World War I the German empire had enlisted medical science as an instrument of aggressive military power by putting it to use in the development of gas warfare. It was left to the Nazi dictatorship to make medical science into an instrument of political power - a formidable, essential tool in the complete and effective manipulation of totalitarian control. This should be a warning to all civilized nations, and particularly to individuals who are blinded by the 'efficiency' of a totalitarian rule, under whatever name.

This entire body of research as reported so far served the master crime to which the Nazi dictatorship was committed - namely, the genocide of non-German peoples and the elimination by killing, in groups or singly, of Germans who were considered useless or disloyal. In effecting the two parts of this program, Himmler demanded and received the co-operation of physicians and of German medical science. The result was a significant advance in the science of killing, or ktenology.

Medicomilitary Research

Another chapter in Nazi scientific research was that aimed
to aid the military forces. Many of these ideas originated
with Himmler, who fancied himself a scientist.

When Himmler learned that the cause of death of most
SS men on the battlefield was hemorrhage, he instructed
Dr Sigmund Rascher to search for a blood coagulant that
might be given before the men went into action. Rascher
tested this coagulant when it was developed by clocking
the number of drops emanating from freshly cut amputation
stumps of living and conscious prisoners at the
crematorium of Dachau concentration camp and by
shooting Russian prisoners of war through the spleen.

Live dissections were a feature of another experimental
study designed to show the effects of explosive
decompression.[12-14] A mobile decompression chamber
was used. It was found that when subjects were made to
descend from altitudes of 40,000 to 60,000 feet without
oxygen, severe symptoms of cerebral dysfunction occurred
- at first convulsions, then unconsciousness in which the
body was hanging limp and later, after wakening,
temporary blindness, paralysis or severe confusional
twilight states. Rascher, who wanted to find out whether
these symptoms were due to anoxic changes or to other
causes, did what appeared to him the most simple thing:
he placed the subjects of the experiment under water and
dissected them while the heart was still beating,
demonstrating air embolism in the blood vessels of the
heart, liver, chest wall and brain.

---

[12]   Alexander, L. Miscellaneous aviation medical matters.
Combined Intelligence Objectives Subcommittee, Item No. 24, File
No. XXIX-21. Pp. 1-163 (August), 1945.
13.   Document 1971 a PS.
14.   Document NO 220.

Another part of Dr Rascher's research, carried out in collaboration with Holzloehner and Finke, concerned shock from exposure to cold.[15]   It was known that military personnel generally did not survive immersion in the North Sea for more than sixty to a hundred minutes. Rascher therefore attempted to duplicate these conditions at Dachau concentration camp and used about 300 prisoners in experiments on shock from exposure to cold; of these 80 to 90 were killed. (The figures do not include persons killed during mass experiments on exposure to cold outdoors.)   In one report on this work Rascher asked permission to shift these experiments from Dachau to Auschwitz, a larger camp where they might cause less disturbance because the subjects shrieked from pain when their extremities froze white. The results, like so many of those obtained in the Nazi research program, are not dependable. In his report Rascher stated that it took from fifty-three to a hundred minutes to kill a human being by immersion in ice water - a time closely in agreement with the known survival period in the North Sea. Inspection of his own experimental records and statements made to me by his close associates showed that it actually took from eighty minutes to five or six hours to kill an undressed person in such a manner, whereas a man in full aviator's dress took six or seven hours to kill. Obviously, Rascher dressed up his findings to forestall criticism, although any scientific man should have known that during actual exposure many other factors, including greater convection of heat due to the motion of water, would affect the time of survival.

Another series of experiments gave results that might have been an important medical contribution if an

15   Alexander, L. Treatment of shock from prolonged exposure to cold, especially in water. Combined Intelligence Objectives Subcommittee, Item No. 24, File No. XXVI-37. Pp. 1-228 (July), 1945.

important lead had not been ignored. The efficacy of various vaccines and drugs against typhus was tested at the Buchenwald and Natzweiler concentration camps. Prevaccinated persons and non-vaccinated controls were injected with live typhus rickettsias, and the death rates of the two series compared. After a certain number of passages, the Matelska strain of typhus rickettsia proved to become avirulent for men. Instead of seizing upon this as a possibility to develop a live vaccine, the experimenters, including the chief consultant, Professor Gerhard Rose, who should have known better, were merely annoyed at the fact that the controls did not die either, discarded this strain and continued testing their relatively ineffective dead vaccines against a new virulent strain. This incident shows that the basic unconscious motivation and attitude has a great influence in determining the scientist's awareness of the phenomena that pass through his vision.

Sometimes human subjects were used for tests that were totally unnecessary, or whose results could have been predicted by simple chemical experiments. For example, 90 gypsies were given unaltered sea water and sea water whose taste was camouflaged as their sole source of fluid, apparently to test the well known fact that such hypertonic saline solutions given as the only source of supply of fluid will cause severe physical disturbance or death within six to twelve days. These persons were subjected to the tortures of the damned, with death resulting in at least 2 cases.

Heteroplastic transplantation experiments were carried out by Professor Dr Karl Gebhardt at Himmler's suggestion. Whole limbs - shoulder, arm or leg - were amputated from live prisoners at Ravensbrueck concentration camp, wrapped in sterile moist dressings and sent by automobile to the SS hospital at Hohenlychen, where Professor Gebhardt busied himself with a futile attempt at heteroplastic transplantation. In the meantime the prisoners deprived of a limb were usually killed by lethal injection.

One would not be dealing with German science if one did not run into manifestations of the collector's spirit. By February 1942, it was assumed in German scientific circles that the Jewish race was about to be completely exterminated, and alarm was expressed over the fact that only very few specimens of skulls and skeletons of Jews were at the disposal of science. It was therefore proposed that a collection of 150 body casts and skeletons of Jews be preserved for perusal by future students of anthropology. Dr August Hirt, professor of anatomy at the University of Strassburg, declared himself interested in establishing such a collection at his anatomic institute. He suggested that captured Jewish officers of the Russian armed forces be included, as well as females from Auschwitz concentration camp; that they be brought alive to Natzweiler concentration camp near Strassburg; and that after 'their subsequently induced death - care should be taken that the heads not be damaged [sic]' the bodies be turned over to him at the anatomic institute of the University of Strassburg. This was done. The entire collection of bodies and the correspondence pertaining to it fell into the hands of the United States Army.

One of the most revolting experiments was the testing of sulfonamides against gas gangrene by Professor Gebhardt and his collaborators, for which young women captured from the Polish Resistance Movement served as subjects. Necrosis was produced in a muscle of the leg by ligation and the wound was infected with various types of gas-gangrene bacilli; frequently, dirt, pieces of wood and glass splinters were added to the wound. Some of these victims died, and others sustained severe mutilating deformities of the leg.

Motivation

An important feature of the experiments performed in concentration camps is the fact that they not only represented a ruthless and callous pursuit of legitimate scientific goals but also were motivated by rather sinister practical ulterior political and personal purposes, arising out of the requirements and problems of the administration of totalitarian rule.

Why did men like Professor Gebhardt lend themselves to such experiments? The reasons are fairly simple and practical, no surprise to anyone familiar with the evidence of fear, hostility, suspicion, rivalry and intrigue, the fratricidal struggle euphemistically termed the 'self-selection of leaders', that went on within the ranks of the ruling Nazi party and the SS. The answer was fairly simple and logical. Dr Gebhardt performed these experiments to clear himself of the suspicion that he had been contributing to the death of SS General Reinhard ('The Hangman') Heydrich, either negligently or deliberately, by failing to treat his wound infection with sulfonamides. After Heydric died from gas gangrene, Himmler himself told Dr Gebhardt that the only way in which he could prove that Heydrich's death was 'fate determined' was by carrying out a 'large-scale experiment' in prisoners, which would prove or disprove that people died from gas gangrene irrespective of whether they were treated with sulfonamides or not.

Dr Sigmund Rascher did not become the notorious vivisectionist of Dachau concentration camp and the willing tool of Himmler's research interests until he had been forbidden to use the facilities of the Pathological Institute of the University of Munich because he was suspected of having Communist sympathies. Then he was ready to go all out and do anything merely to regain acceptance by the Nazi party and the SS.

These cases illustrate a method consciously and methodically used in the SS, an age-old method used by criminal gangs everywhere: that of making suspects of disloyalty clear themselves by participation in a crime that would definitely and irrevocably tie them to the organization. In the SS this process of reinforcement of group cohesion was called 'Blutkitt' (blood-cement), a term that Hitler himself is said to have obtained from a book on Genghis Khan in which this technic was emphasized.

The important lesson here is that this motivation with which one is familiar in ordinary crimes, applies also to war crimes and to ideologically conditioned crimes against humanity - namely, that fear and cowardice, especially fear of punishment or of ostracism by the group, are often more important motives than simple ferocity or aggressiveness.

The Early Change in Medical Attitudes

Whatever proportions these crimes finally assumed, it became evident to all who investigated them that they had started from small beginnings. The beginnings at first were merely a subtle shift in emphasis in the basic attitude of the physicians. It started with the acceptance of the attitude, basic in the euthanasia movement, that there is such a thing as life not worthy to be lived. This attitude in its early stages concerned itself merely with the severely and chronically sick. Gradually the sphere of those to be included in this category was enlarged to encompass the socially unproductive, the ideologically unwanted, the racially unwanted and finally all non-Germans. But it is important to realize that the infinitely small wedged-in lever from which this entire trend of mind received its impetus was the attitude toward the nonrehabilitable sick.

It is, therefore, this subtle shift in emphasis of the physician's attitude that one must thoroughly investigate. It is a recent significant trend in medicine, including psychiatry, to regard prevention as more important than cure. Observation and recognition of early signs and symptoms have become the basis for prevention of further advance of disease.8

In looking for these early signs one may well retrace the early steps of propaganda on the part of the Nazis in Germany as well as in the countries that they overran and in which they attempted to gain supporters by means of indoctrination, seduction and propaganda.

The Example of Successful Resistance by the Physicians of the Netherlands

There is no doubt that in Germany itself the first and most effective step of propaganda within the medical profession was the propaganda barrage against the useless, incurably sick described above. Similar, even more subtle efforts were made in some of the occupied countries. It is to the everlasting honor of the medical profession of Holland that they recognized the earliest and most subtle phases of this attempt and rejected it. When Seiss-Inquart, Reich Commissar for the Occupied Netherlands Territories, wanted to draw the Dutch physicians into the orbit of the activities of the German medical profession, he did not tell them 'You must send your chronic patients to death factories' or 'You must give lethal injections at Government request in your offices', but he couched his order in most careful and superficially acceptable terms. One of the paragraphs in the order of the Reich Commissar of the Netherlands Territories concerning the Netherlands doctors of 19 December 1941 reads as follows: 'It is the duty of the doctor, through advice and effort, conscientiously and to his best ability, to assist as helper the person entrusted to his care in the maintenance, improvement and re-establishment of his vitality, physical efficiency and health. The accomplishment of this duty is a public task.'[16]   The physicians of Holland rejected this order unanimously because they saw what it actually meant - namely, the concentration of their efforts on mere rehabilitation of the sick for useful labor, and abolition of medical secrecy. Although on the surface the new order appeared not too grossly unacceptable, the Dutch physicians decided that it is the first, although slight, step away from principle that is the most important one. The Dutch physicians declared that they would not obey this order. When Seiss-Inquart threatened them with revocation of their licenses, they returned their licenses, removed their shingles and, while seeing their own patients secretly, no longer wrote death or birth certificates. Seiss-Inquart retraced his steps and tried to cajole them - still to no effect. Then he arrested 100 Dutch physicians and sent them to concentration camps. The medical profession remained adamant and quietly took care of their widows and orphans, but would not give in. Thus it came about that not a single euthanasia or non-therapeutic sterilization was recommended or participated in by any Dutch physician. They had the foresight to resist before the first step was taken, and they acted unanimously and won out in the end. It is obvious that if the medical profession of a small nation under the conqueror's heel could resist so effectively the German medical profession could likewise have resisted had they not taken the fatal first step. It is the first seemingly innocent step away from principle that frequently decides a career of crime. Corrosion begins in microscopic proportions.

---

[16]   Seiss-Inquart. Order of the Reich Commissar for the Occupied Netherlands Territories Concerning the Netherlands Doctors. (Gazette containing the orders for the Occupied Netherlands Territories), pp. 1004-1026, December, 1941.

The Situation in the United States

The question that this fact prompts is whether there are
any danger signs that American physicians have also been
infected with Hegelian, cold-blooded, utilitarian philosophy
and whether early traces of it can be detected in their
medical thinking that may make them vulnerable to
departures of the type that occurred in Germany. Basic
attitudes must be examined dispassionately. The original
concept of medicine and nursing was not based on any
rational or feasible likelihood that they could actually cure
and restore but rather on an essentially maternal or
religious idea. The Good Samaritan had no thought of nor
did he actually care whether he could restore working
capacity. He was merely motivated by the compassion in
alleviating suffering. Bernal[17] states that prior to the
advent of scientific medicine, the physician's main function
was to give hope to the patient and to relieve his relatives
of responsibility. Gradually, in all civilized countries,
medicine has moved away from this position, strangely
enough in direct proportion to man's actual ability to
perform feats that would have been plain miracles in days
of old. However, with this increased efficiency based on
scientific development went a subtle change in attitude.
Physicians have become dangerously close to being mere
technicians of rehabilitation. This essentially Hegelian
rational attitude has led them to make certain distinctions
in the handling of acute and chronic diseases. The patient
with the latter carries an obvious stigma as the one less
likely to be fully rehabilitable for social usefulness. In an
increasingly utilitarian society these patients are being
looked down upon with increasing definiteness as
unwanted ballast. A certain amount of rather open
contempt for the people who cannot be rehabilitated with
present knowledge has developed. This is probably due to
a good deal of unconscious hostility, because these people

---

[17]   Bernal, J.D. *The Social Function of Science*. Sixth edition.
482 pp. London: George Routledge & Sons, 1946.

for whom there seem to be no effective remedies have become a threat to newly acquired delusions of omnipotence.

Hospitals like to limit themselves to the care of patients who can be fully rehabilitated, and the patient whose full rehabilitation is unlikely finds himself, at least in the best and most advanced centers of healing, as a second-class patient faced with a reluctance on the part of both the visiting and the house staff to suggest and apply therapeutic procedures that are not likely to bring about immediately striking results in terms of recovery. I wish to emphasize that this point of view did not arise primarily within the medical profession, which has always been outstanding in a highly competitive economic society for giving freely and unstintingly of its time and efforts, but was imposed by the shortage of funds available, both private and public. From the attitude of easing patients with chronic diseases away from the doors of the best types of treatment facilities available to the actual dispatching of such patients to killing centers is a long but nevertheless logical step. Resources for the so-called incurable patient have recently become practically unavailable.

There has never in history been a shortage of money for the development and manufacture of weapons of war; there is and should be none now. The disproportion of monetary support for war and that available for healing and care is an anachronism in an era that has been described as the 'enlightened age of the common man' by some observers. The comparable cost of jet planes and hospital beds is too obvious for any excuse to be found for a shortage of the latter. I trust that these remarks will not be misunderstood. I believe that armament, including jet planes, is vital for the security of the republic, but adequate maintenance of standards of health and alleviation of suffering are equally vital, both from a practical point of view and from that of morale. All who took part in induction-board examinations during the war realize that the maintenance and development of national health is of as vital importance as the maintenance and development of armament.

The trend of development in the facilities available for the chronically ill outlined above will not necessarily be altered by public or state medicine. With provision of public funds in any setting of public activity the question is bound to come up, 'Is it worth while to spend a certain amount of effort to restore a certain type of patient?' This rationalistic point of view has insidiously crept into the motivation of medical effort, supplanting the old Hippocratic point of view. In emergency situations, military or otherwise, such grading of effort may be pardonable. But doctors must beware lest such attitudes creep into the civilian public administration of medicine entirely outside emergency situations, because once such considerations are at all admitted, the more often and the more definitely the question is going to be asked, 'Is it worth while to do this or that for this type of patient?' Evidence of the existence of such an attitude stared at me from a report on the activities of a leading public hospital unit, which stated rather proudly that certain treatments were given only when they appeared promising: 'Our facilities are such that a case load of 20 patients is regularly carried . . . in selecting cases for treatment careful consideration is given to the prognostic criteria, and in no instance have we instituted treatment merely to satisfy relatives or our own consciences.' If only those whose treatment is worth while in terms of prognosis are to be treated, what about the other ones whose recovery appears unlikely, but frequently if treated energetically, they surprise the best prognosticators. And what shall be done during that long time lag after the disease has been called incurable and the time of death and autopsy? It is that period during which it is most difficult to find hospitals and other therapeutic organizations for the welfare and alleviation of suffering of the patient.

Under all forms of dictatorship the dictating bodies or individuals claim that all that is done is being done for the best of the people as a whole, and for that reason they look at health merely in terms of utility, efficiency and productivity. It is natural in such a setting that eventually Hegel's principle that 'what is useful is good' wins out completely. The killing center is the *reductio ad absurdum* of all health planning based only on rational principles and economy and not on humane compassion and divine law. To be sure, American physicians are still far from the point of thinking of killing centers, but they have arrived at a danger point in thinking, at which likelihood of full rehabilitation is considered a factor that should determine the amount of time, effort and cost to be devoted to a particular type of patient on the part of the social body upon which this decision rests. At this point Americans should remember that the enormity of a euthanasia movement is present in their own minds. To the psychiatrist it is obvious that this represents the eruption of unconscious aggression on the part of certain administrators alluded to above, as well as on the part of relatives who have been understandably frustrated by the tragedy of illness in its close interaction upon their own lives. The hostility of a father erupting against his feebleminded son is understandable and should be considered from the psychiatric point of view, but it certainly should not influence social thinking. The development of effective analgesics and pain-relieving operations has taken even the last rationalization away from the supporters of euthanasia.

The case, therefore, that I should like to make is that American medicine must realize where it stands in its fundamental premises. There can be no doubt that in a subtle way the Hegelian premise of 'what is useful is right'

has infected society, including the medical portion.
Physicians must return to the older premises, which were
the emotional foundation and driving force of an amazingly
successful quest to increase powers of healing and which
are bound to carry them still farther if they are not held
down to earth by the pernicious attitudes of an overdone
practical realism.

What occurred in Germany may have been the
inexorable historic progression that the Greek historians
have described as the law of the fall of civilizations and
that Toynbee[18] has convincingly confirmed - namely, that
there is a logical sequence from Koros to Hybris to Ate,
which means from surfeit to disdainful arrogance to
disaster, the surfeit being increased scientific and practical
accomplishments, which, however, brought about an
inclination to throw away the old motivations and values
by disdainful arrogant pride in practical efficiency. Moral
and physical disaster is the inevitable consequence.

Fortunately, there are developments in this democratic
society that counteract these trends. Notable among them
are the societies of patients afflicted with various chronic
diseases that have sprung up and are dedicating
themselves to guidance and information for their fellow
sufferers and for the support and stimulation of medical
research. Among the earliest was the mental-hygiene
movement, founded by a former patient with mental
disease. Then came the National Foundation for Infantile
Paralysis, the tuberculosis societies, the American
Epilepsy League, the National Association to Control
Epilepsy, the American Cancer Society, The American
Heart Association, 'Alcoholics Anonymous' and, most
recently, the National Multiple Sclerosis Society. All these

---

18   Toynbee, A.J. *A Study of History*. Abridgement of Vol. I-
VI. By D.C. Somervell. 617 pp. New York and London: Oxford
University Press, 1947.

societies, which are co-ordinated with special medical societies and which received inspiration and guidance from outstanding physicians, are having an extremely wholesome effect in introducing fresh motivating power into the ivory towers of academic medicine. It is indeed interesting and an assertion of democratic vitality that these societies are activated by and for people suffering from illnesses who, under certain dictatorships, would have been slated for euthanasia.

It is thus that these new societies have taken over one of the ancient functions of medicine - namely, to give hope to the patient and to relieve his relatives. These societies need the whole-hearted support of the medical profession. Unfortunately, this support is by no means yet unanimous. A distinguished physician, investigator and teacher at an outstanding university recently told me that he was opposed to these special societies and clinics because they had nothing to offer to the patient. It would be better to wait until someone made a discovery accidentally and then start clinics. It is my opinion, however, that one cannot wait for that. The stimulus supplied by these societies is necessary to give stimulus both to public demand and to academic medicine, which at times grows stale and unproductive even in its most outstanding centers, and whose existence did nothing to prevent the executioner from having logic on his side in Germany.

Another element of this free democratic society and enterprise that has been a stimulus to new developments is the pharmaceutical industry, which, with great vision, has invested considerable effort in the sponsorship of new research.

Dictatorships can be indeed defined as systems in which there is a prevalence of thinking in destructive rather than in ameliorative terms in dealing with social problems. The ease with which destruction of life is advocated for those

considered either socially useless or socially disturbing
instead of educational or ameliorative measures may be
the first danger sign of loss of creative liberty in thinking,
which is the hallmark of democratic society. All
destructiveness ultimately leads to self-destruction; the
fate of the SS and of Nazi Germany is an eloquent
example. The destructive principle, once unleashed, is
bound to engulf the whole personality and to occupy all its
relationships. Destructive urges and destructive concepts
arising therefrom cannot remain limited or focused upon
one subject or several subjects alone, but must inevitably
spread and be directed against one's entire surrounding
world, including one's own group and ultimately the self.
The ameliorative point of view maintained in relation to all
others is the only real means of self-preservation.

A most important need in this country is for the
development of active and alert hospital centers for the
treatment of chronic illnesses. They must have active
staffs similar to those of the hospitals for acute illnesses,
and these hospitals must be fundamentally different from
the custodial repositories for derelicts, of which there are
too many in existence today. Only thus can one give the
right answer to divine scrutiny: Yes, we are our brothers'
keepers.

3

Theological Perspectives on Euthanasia

Nigel M. de S. Cameron

Introduction

Any proper development of a Christian theological perspective on death and dying must be worked out in counterpoint with the questions of health and healing. Many of the ills that may be diagnosed in contemporary understanding in both these areas are the result of a failure to maintain the connexion.

The current rising tide of interest in healing across a wide spectrum of Christian and other opinion must always be open to the criticism that it does not pay due regard to the final context of human life. We must take up a position from which both health and healing, and death and dying, can be held in focus from a single point.

Curiously, an over-concern with healing has unpredictable effects for our thinking about dying. It may be cognate with a respect for the person which will lead in turn to a proper perception of what is a dignified human death. Conversely, it can - and does - lead to the pernicious notion that the only human life worth calling a human life is *mens sana in corpore sano,* and vigorously so too. The only dignified death is as speedy a move as possible from such healthy living to the grave.

Yet, I would suggest, the only truly healthy mind is one which has come to terms with the fact that healthy bodies are ephemeral things, that 'all flesh is grass', and that human dignity transcends both healthiness and all the other accompaniments of well-being in this life. The greatness, and the endless vigour, of the Christian view of man lies in its regard for his life here below, and its equal disregard of its finality. Male and female, human creatures, we are made in the image of God. But we look to the resurrection of the dead, and the life of the world to come.

Now that is the context in which we must set a theological reflection on the subject of euthanasia. It is altogether wider than the particular issue in which it tends to be focussed - the care of the sick. Specifically *theological* reflection sheds light on the ethical questions raised by the idea of 'euthanasia' precisely by standing back and asking not, 'How should man die?', but 'What is man?', and 'What, therefore, is the nature of the human condition in which we experience both life and death?' It resolutely avoids the naive isolation of terminal care from these prior questions.

Our society gives these questions answers which are increasingly confused and uncertain; so that the once firm consensus on what is a dignified death has grown fragile. We have first to answer the question, 'What is a dignified life?' It is the isolation of the question of death and dying from other human questions that helps lead us into the blind alley of a programme of euthanasia. In euthanasia we see the final denial of a dignified death, and the triumph of the principles of veterinary medicine over the Hippocratic tradition; not that there is anything wrong with veterinary medicine, but it is a medicine appropriate to its subjects. If the medicine of Hippocrates and our western Christian tradition is to survive, it can never lose sight of who we are, we who are its patients and its practitioners. That is why the question of what man is, and what is a dignified life, are so central. We cannot speak of the management of the dying process until we have asked who it is who is dying. If it is a horse, then let the vet have his way and treat his patient as a horse. But if a man, then let him be treated as a man. Yet, we ask, *what is a man*? In what particular does he differ from a horse?

Some of us believe that our medical tradition is in process of transformation into a new medicine whose ethical character - indeed, whose entire character - is altogether different. And why? Because - if we may put it like this - we have begun to forget who we are. We do not know who we are. The collective amnesia of the once-Christian West may itself prove irreversible and, if it does, it is hard to believe that it will not finally prove a terminal condition for our society.[1]

1. The patient: a Christian view of life and death
If we may put it in a sentence, the Christian view of man is that he is the glory of creation, but sullied and tainted by an all but fatal fallenness that corrupted the race in its first beginnings, and corrupts it still. Death, whatever else it is, is the wages of sin, and as such not just an indignity but an affront, to man and to God; the 'last enemy', in the presence of which our Lord himself wept. We live as we die, under the curse that is God's reflex to sin. Yet we live also in a day of grace, whose first announcement in the midst of the curse itself (the so-called protevangelium) sets the double context of our human experience as both

---

[1].This is the theme of my book *The New Medicine* , forthcoming from Hodder & Stoughton.

curse and blessing, a bitter-sweet sampling of the moral character of the universe itself, a cockpit of the struggle of good and evil in which the transcendent triumph of the grace and goodness of God may take on the hiddenness of the cross; and in which the biblical refrains of 'Why do the wicked prosper?', and 'How long, O Lord, how long?', are the bread and butter of our nights and our days.

For hiddenness and ambiguity mark all the dealings of God with his world. In every day Job will have his comforters, who in all pious conscience believe they can read the mind of God off the pages of our history, as if every man were a prophet. The prosperity preachers of health and wealth are but the latest in a long line, whose concept of the prosperity which God gives to his children has been hammered into a shallowness of this-worldly proportion. And if you scratch the surface of many a Christian, you will find another. We sing:

> Blind unbelief is sure to err
> And scan his work in vain;
> God is his own interpreter,
> And he will make it plain.

Which means two things: the eye of faith can never rest on appearances; and our acceptance in faith of the ambiguous character of our human experience and the hiddenness of God's purposes is an acceptance for this life only. He *will* make it plain: explanation is eschatological - it belongs to the winding up of human affairs, the dawning of the world to come, and the vision of God in the final realisation of the goal of human experience. Until then, its burdensome character, which reaches and sometimes crosses the margins of the intolerable, must remain without the kind of answers Job sought - and his comforters deceived themselves into thinking they had discovered.

But if man is the glory of creation, the chief among the works of God, destined for an eternity of glory or shame and set in a space-time matrix of judgement and grace, blessing and curse - if *that* is who he is, how is he to assess the possibilities of life and death when the scale-pan is heavy with trouble?

There are of course examples in Holy Scripture of men who have sought escape - what has been curiously termed self-deliverance, though a deliverance only from the frying pan. Their examples, if only tangentially relevant to our present discussion, are in any event unencouraging. In the New Testament we have Judas who, unable to live with the remorse of betrayal, hanged himself. In the Old, coming a little closer to the matter in hand, we have King Saul; who, facing the death of his sons, defeat in battle and the prospect of capture, fails to secure the assistance in suicide of his servant, falls on his sword, and seeks aid from a passing Amalekite to finish him off. The Amalekite proves more amenable than his servant, though from motives undoubtedly mixed, but receives his own reward from David, to whom he breaks the news of his hand in the slaying of Saul, and who has him dispatched in turn.

But we come closer to the contemporary question of euthanasia by returning to Job, for Job is presented to us as a potential volunteer. His children are dead, his wealth is gone, and his quality of life is evidently ebbing, since he finds himself covered with boils from head to toe. His wife shows herself an early recruit to the movement for voluntary euthanasia. 'Curse God and die', she recommends her husband (2:9). He is of another mind: 'You are talking like a foolish woman', he retorts; 'shall we accept good from God and not trouble?' (2:10). Yet his anguish is great, he feels himself to have trespassed beyond the bounds of the tolerable, and he cries out to God: 'Why is light given to those in misery and life to the bitter of soul, to those who long for death that does not

come, who search for it more than for hidden treasure, who
are filled with gladness when they reach the grave?' (3:20-
3).

And if you know Job, you know that is but a sample of
his wrestling with the intolerable. Yet it is characterised,
from the start, by his acceptance of, as it were, the
ground-rules of providence; and of the fact that, come what
may, he stands ever before God. God does not at this time
deliver him from his circumstances; nor does his resolute
faith enable him to discount them. It is in the intolerable
anguish of his near-despair that Job's faith is tried. Job
remembers who he is as he is reminded who is his God.
His motto could have been something that one of my
daughters said to me when she was three years old, and
frightened of the dark. 'It doesn't matter if it's dark, does it,
Daddy, because it's *meant* to be dark.'

So, first of all I would suggest to you that death casts its
long shadow right across the face of human experience.
There is no pleasure, no achievement, no single episode in
the human story that escapes its sober shade. Even the
marriage ceremony rightly reminds us that our temporal
joys will one day dissolve in the final parting. Now, the
person who has not laid hold on that sombre truth knows
as little about life as he does about death. If we find in it a
surd and ultimately intolerable quality, we should not be
surprised. If, like Job, we have learned to bring the
intolerable to God - and if in Jesus Christ we have found
him to share it with us - we have grasped something of
the life of faith.

The context in which we view human life - in its dignity
and indignity, its pleasure and its pain, its sickness and
finally its dissolution in death - is sombre, and yet it is
realistic. We are thereby preserved from any notion of
health and vigour as other than one temporary aspect of
what it is to be human in a fallen world, and we are

encouraged to view its absence - whether in handicap or sickness - in an altogether different manner. For the answer we have forgotten to the question we do not ask is that man is made in the very image of God. Distinct from every other creature, man is made to be like God. The sacredness of his life arises out of his being as like his maker as God could make any creature. Created human nature is of such an awesome dignity that God himself can choose to make it his own in Jesus Christ - and to retain it, even now and forever, in a glorified humanity which is human nonetheless. The sanctity of human life is a non-negotiable of the biblical view of man, underlined rather than undermined by the exceptions to which Scripture itself adverts - self-defence, the capital sentence, and just warfare.

The medicalising of the context makes no difference to the character of the intentional killing of the patient (with or without consent, by omission or commission), just as it makes no difference to the relation of doctor to patient as that of one citizen to another. Holy Scripture so defines the dignity of man the image-bearer as to exclude the taking of his life, and at a time when the management options open to those caring for the sick and the dying were immeasurably fewer.

2. The doctor: a Christian view of medicine
I do not wish to trespass into the territory of the other contributors, but it is necessary to say this much in order to underline the antipathy of a coherent view of the medical enterprise for medical killing. The debate has suffered from the terminology which has often been its currency. The claim that euthanasia represents 'death with dignity' is firmly challenged by the question-mark in the title of this conference, *Death with Dignity?* But why 'euthanasia', a good or easy death, as if no other death were good or easy? And as if this one were? 'Euthanasia' has no distinct place in our law, and we must constantly challenge the

widespread assumption that it has in our ethics. It is a euphemism for one of a number of varieties of homicide, the killing of one person by another. It is not simply 'assisted suicide', though that were discreditable enough. It is homicide, whether or not at the instigation or with the consent of its victim. Even when supposedly 'voluntary' (and the apologists of euthanasia need to ask much harder questions about the 'voluntary' character of the volunteer's choice if they are to carry credibility as the apostles of patient autonomy) - even then, the act is homicide. We must explode the myth that it is some kind of 'third thing', somehow mid-way between homicide and a natural death. Indeed, there is this to be said for the term 'mercy-killing', that it retains the essential character of the act as an act of *killing,* while recognising the special motivation alleged to be present. This term also has the advantage that it is less easy to qualify it with the weasel-word 'voluntary'.

And it is because euthanasia is the killing of the patient that this represents so fundamental a challenge to our medical tradition. Because the roots of the tradition in the ancient medicine of Hippocrates made a distinction, for the first time in our culture - according to Margaret Mead - between 'curing' and 'killing'; a pair of terms interestingly taken up, whether by accident or design, in the BMA Report. Euthanasia involves the physician in neither of his accustomed roles of healing and palliative care, but in entering the Hippocratic exclusion zone where killing is done in the name of medicine.

But what is a Christian view of medicine, a theological perspective on the healing arts? I suggest to you that the role of the physician, as a healer, may best be understood as eschatological. Once again, we must look at this life in the context of the life to come. I think we err in setting too wide a division between the healing of the physician's natural skills and the supernatural healing of miracle, exemplified in the ministry of our Lord. Both alike point forward, both are anticipations in the here and now of that most distinctly Christian of eschatological blessings, the resurrection of the body. If, as I have suggested, this life is a preparation for death, lived out under its shadow, it is also in turn a preparation for the resurrection of the dead; and the practice of healing, whether by nature or supernature, is a sampling process of that blessed state. Medicine is called into a constant and finally unsuccessful struggle with the reign of death over fallen human existence. The physician - and this surely and rightly explains something of the awe in which he is held - the physician is an agent of the world to come; and whenever the sick are raised up or the pain and distress of the chronically or terminally ill are held at bay, it is nothing other than the power of the resurrection which is at work.

Now you must forgive me for offering you a theology of medicine in a paragraph. But it enables me to go on to conclude how singularly incoherent would be a healer as an agent of something other than healing. The incongruity of the physician as an agent of death could hardly be greater.

And that is why I think it is important to grasp the great gulf that is fixed between the advocacy of euthanasia and the Hippocratic and Judaeo-Christian medical tradition. For euthanasia - the taking up of killing again, alongside curing, into the practice of medicine - represents so fundamental a departure from the ethical framework of humane medicine that it requires the re-structuring of that framework along lines that must ultimately prove profoundly different. A new medicine is arising to challenge, and to seek to displace, the old, with in the place of healing as its supreme objective a fluid and undefined notion of the relief of suffering - which can encompass even the taking of life. This new medicine is no Christian medicine. It imparts no dignity to death since it recognises no final dignity in life. Though their motives may be the best, and their integrity beyond question, its advocates are the product of the post-Christian world, and it is a post-Christian medicine. Much, indeed, it retains in common with the tradition out of which it has come. But much of this continues not because of, but despite, its true character.

For at heart, this is not a debate about the proper management of chronic and terminal illness; it is that only in passing. It is a debate about the nature of man, the nature of medicine and - ultimately - the nature of God himself.

4

Euthanasia: Some Points in a Philosophical Polemic

Luke Gormally

The following text is a very lightly revised version of the talk I gave at the Conference on 11 March 1989. I have included a section which had to be omitted on that occasion because of shortage of time, and have added some endnotes. I am grateful for advice in revising the text to John Finnis, to my colleagues Fred Fitzpatrick and Agneta Sutton, and especially to Mary Geach.

In most societies there is an admixture of civilisation and barbarism: the legal and political institutions of a society more or less adequately embody recognition of those principles which help to secure ways of living consistent with human dignity and the destiny of man. But every society falls short of securing, in its governance of human relationships, that every human being be protected against arbitrary exercises of power.

Our society is well-advanced on the road to systematic rejection of principles for the protection of human life which rest on a recognition of the dignity of *every* human being. This rejection is most conspicuously embodied in the legalisation and widespread practice of abortion, and in a defence policy, adopted on our behalf by successive British governments, which depends on the conditional intention to murder innocent civilians. I shall argue in this paper that acceptance of the practice of voluntary euthanasia in our society would be a significant futher step in the direction of barbarism, *i.e.,* a state of affairs in which human beings, at times of great vulnerability, are no longer protected by the canons of justice, but are increasingly at the mercy of the arbitrary exercise of power. Civil authority, of course, exists to prevent this, not to promote it.

Every Christian has a vocation to witness to that truth about man which is knowable through the works of creation as well as that which is revealed in the word of God. In face of the contemporary assault on human dignity it is urgent that Christians collaborate in so far as they can in this task of witness.

My assignment, however, is not that of reflecting on revealed truths - the theological task undertaken by Dr Cameron [1] - but of offering on the topic of euthanasia some reflections which one would hope any man of good will could recognise as true without the benefit of revelation. The philosophical literature on euthanasia is beginning to be voluminous, so I shall have to be very selective about the points I cover in the time at my disposal. I have confined myself to a limited number of points in what one might call a philosophical polemic against euthanasia. In consequence a number of important issues are not addressed.

I shall begin by focusing on *voluntary* euthanasia, partly because the legalisation of voluntary euthanasia is the immediate objective of the euthanasia movement. I shall seek to identify the fundamental reason which is made to bear the burden of justifying the killing of patients who ask for euthanasia. I will then go on to ask whether this is an acceptable reason for killing people, and whether as a society we can accommodate such killing consistent with the fundamental assumptions of our legal system. I shall argue that we cannot, and that not even the high value placed on autonomy in the liberal political tradition provides reason for legalising voluntary euthanasia. Finally, I offer some reflections on the effect the practice of euthanasia would have on the practice of medicine.

Let me begin by defining what I mean by 'voluntary euthanasia'. By 'voluntary euthanasia' I mean the intentional causing of a patient's death or, more plainly, the intentional killing of a patient in the course of medical care, when the killing is carried out at the patient's request, and the patient is believed by a doctor to have good reason *to be killed* because of his or her present or foreseeable mental condition and quality of life.

There are four elements to this definition of voluntary euthanasia.

1. First it involves *intentional killing:* in other words a doctor aims to bring about a patient's death either by something he does - for example, by a lethal injection of a toxic substance - or by something he deliberately omits to do precisely with a view to bringing about death.[2] He may, for example, fail to give a patient the nutrition she needs precisely in order to bring about her death; in other words, he may starve her to death (this is done to handicapped babies). Or he may withhold necessary life-prolonging treatment, which he had an obligation to provide, precisely in order to bring about death. So one can intentionally kill

someone by deliberate omissions - by deliberate failures to act - just as much as by positive deeds. We should be clear that, in one way or another, euthanasia involves intentional killing. Euphemisms like 'easing the passing' and 'helping to die' are linguistic devices of the devil (or Orwellian 'newspeak') designed to prevent clear thinking. [3]

2. The second element in the definition of voluntary euthanasia is that the killing of the patient is *in the course of medical care*. Clearly people *other* than doctors can kill patients for euthanasiast reasons. But proponents of voluntary euthanasia are particularly interested in having doctors kill patients *as an accepted part of clinical practice*. If we may judge by the evolution of abortion practice, it seems clear that nurses will come to be expected to play a prominent role in the execution of euthanasia.

3. The third element in the definition of voluntary euthanasia is that the killing is carried out at the patient's request. Proponents of voluntary euthanasia place great emphasis on the importance of the free, rational choice of the patient; and some of them insist that they have no wish to promote non–voluntary euthanasia (*i.e.*, the killing of patients - like babies - incapable of giving consent) or involuntary euthanasia (*i.e.*, the killing of patients contrary to their wills). But whatever the present attitudes of some proponents of voluntary euthanasia, I shall argue that if there are good grounds for regarding it as acceptable clinical practice then the most important objection to non–voluntary and involuntary euthanasia will have been undermined.

4. The fourth and final element in the definition of euthanasia is that the patient is believed by a doctor to have good reason to be killed because of his or her present or foreseeable mental condition and quality of life.

The existence of the request suggests that the *patient* believes she has good reason to be killed by a doctor. But it is the doctor who is to do the killing. It is the doctor, therefore, who needs to be satisfied that he has good reason to kill the patient.

Requests for euthanasia, as is well known, may be prompted by a patient's erroneous view of her prognosis, or by depression that a doctor can readily see to be transient. So it is quite common for doctors who have no principled objection to euthanasia nonetheless to reject such requests. The mere fact of a request cannot itself provide a good reason for carrying out euthanasia.

Some requests, however, seem to proponents of voluntary euthanasia to be rational, and to provide good reasons for doctors to kill patients. Typically they have in mind the kind of patient who finds intolerable her extensive physical degeneration, perhaps involving immobility, and double incontinence. Her sense of worth and dignity had perhaps been closely tied up throughout her life with the independence she has enjoyed. Extreme dependence on carers makes life seem no longer worthwhile.

There is a variety of conditions which can lead some people to think they no longer have worthwhile lives, and thus lead them to want others to end their lives. Does a patient's present or future quality of life provide a doctor - or, as it may come to be, a nurse - with good reason for killing that patient? Further, is it the kind of reason which our society should recognise as acceptable, either through a reform of the law designed to legalise voluntary euthanasia, or through the acceptance of a code of practice conformity to which on the part of a doctor carrying out euthanasia would ensure freedom from prosecution? These are the key questions.

Throughout the history of human societies certain types
of killing have been thought to be justified. In the Western
tradition of common morality, which has been deeply
influenced by Jewish and Christian moral norms, a
distinction is made between justified and unjustified
killing. This distinction is fundamental to the legal
framework of our societies, and in particular to the criminal
law protecting the lives of all citizens.

Underpinning the traditional distinction between justified
and unjustified killing is the belief that all human beings
are *equal in dignity*. What makes us equal in dignity is
simply our humanity: all that we have in common is the
fact that each of us is a human being. We vary enormously
in capacities and achievements. But our fundamental rights
do not depend on how well-endowed with talents we are
nor on the level of ability we achieve. Unless it is the case
that there is *a basic dignity attaching to our humanity* then
it becomes a matter of choice whom we treat in accordance
with the requirements of justice. If human dignity is not
believed to attach to our humanity but is made to be a
matter of ability or achievement or a particular quality of
life, then we hand a *carte blanche* to the powerful to define
which lives are worthy of protection and which are not.

A society which wants to uphold justice in the treatment
of *all* its members needs above all to hold on to an
understanding of the fundamental dignity of *every* human
being, and to resist any changes which would in practice
subvert that understanding.

The long-established belief that some forms of killing
are morally acceptable relies on justifications consistent
with upholding the dignity of *every* human being, whatever
his or her conditions or circumstances. For the defence of
killing in a just war, justly conducted, and the defence of
capital punishment, after a properly conducted trial, rely on
the proposition that those to be killed must *in some sense*

deserve death. Now there are those who believe that death can never truly be deserved, as well as those who, while holding that it might in principle be deserved, object that it is not deserved by most soldiers in the army of an unjust aggressor or by certain criminals found guilty of capital offences. But the important point to grasp for present purposes in considering the question of whether there ever can be justified intentional killing is this: the traditional defence of some forms of killing does *not* serve to undermine human dignity. Paradoxically, as it may seem, it assumes a very strong belief in human dignity. Only a man who *knowingly* and *willingly* does grave wrong can be held answerable for it and can be said to deserve death. On the traditional view of human dignity, human beings have a special dignity precisely because of the capacity inherent in human nature for knowing the difference between good and evil and for freely choosing which to do.

Now let us remind ourselves again what is involved in voluntary euthanasia. One person, a patient, asks another person, a doctor, to kill him or her. The mere fact of the patient's asking does not provide a good reason for complying with the request. What is supposed to provide a good reason is a patient's well-founded claim that she is suffering or expects to suffer serious degeneration, together with the belief that this degeneration is intolerable and incompatible with her sense of having a worthwhile life, a life of dignity as she has understood it. Such a patient has come to the view that she no longer has a worthwhile life, that such natural life as may be left to her will be devoid of dignity.

There are two questions for a doctor confronted with such a request. The first is: Is he prepared to agree that his patient, and other patients, have not got worthwhile lives, that their lives are devoid of dignity? The second question is: Does he think the judgement that a patient has not got a worthwhile life justifies him in killing that patient?

If the doctor is ready to say 'Yes' to the first question then he has, as far as *belief* is concerned, jettisoned what is essential to the foundations of justice in our society: for the foundations of justice, as we have seen, rest on the belief that *every* human being, just in virtue of being human, possesses an inalienable dignity. And that dignity stands in the way of one human being ever killing another for reasons other than the requirements of justice; that is for reasons which amount to a denial of the human dignity of that human being.

If a doctor says 'Yes' to the second question and acts on that 'Yes', in other words if he kills a patient because he agrees that she has not got a worthwhile life, then in the most decisive way possible he has made his own the view that not every human being enjoys a dignity which prevents us disposing of his or her life for reasons of convenience.

It is clear, I think, that what has to bear the burden of *justifying* killing in voluntary euthanasia is the judgement that a patient lacks a worthwhile life, lacks value. If you subscribe to that judgement you effectively *deny* that every human being has an inalienable dignity just in virtue of his or her humanity.

Members of the euthanasia movement are more or less clear-headed in recognising that the justification even of voluntary euthanasia rests ultimately on the claim that some lives lack value. I have elsewhere published an analysis, which I shall not even summarise here, of the false understanding and false valuation of human life which underpins the euthanasia movement.[4] What I am now concerned to draw attention to is that propagandists for euthanasia require us to jettison what is indisputably fundamental to the legal framework of our society: the view that all men are equal in dignity.

Members of the euthanasia movement are not all clear-headed about the implications of their position. Some are disinclined to acknowledge that the justification of the killing they wish to see carried out in clinical practice must be a judgement on the value or worthwhileness of the patient's life. They protest that the doctor is merely accepting the patient's valuation of her own life.[5] But the question which has to be answered is: Is the doctor *right* to accept that valuation, and so to kill the patient? One reason why some people clearly think that such a doctor would be right is because they believe that human life has indeed no *given*, objective value; the value of each human life is to be determined by each individual human being. The belief of many euthanasiasts about a patient requesting euthanasia is that, 'If she says her life is worthless then it is worthless'.

It is not necessary for present purposes to show why that view is gravely mistaken. I merely draw your attention to two of its implications. First, were the view taken really seriously in the practice of medicine it would leave psychiatrists with little reason for seeking to prevent suicides. The second and more important implication is that if we have not got an objective worth given with our humanity then all men are not equal in dignity. Do people in our society wish to embrace such a view?

Since the real onus for justifying voluntary euthanasia is borne by the judgement that a patient has not got a worthwhile life, it is clear why voluntary euthanasia is a half-way house to non-voluntary and involuntary euthanasia. If a sufficiently powerful and influential group can define some people in society as lacking worthwhile lives, what good reason is there to prevent the killing of those unfortunates? No doubt there are some people in the voluntary euthanasia movement who wish to halt at the half-way house; but there are others who want to move on to the elimination of the senile, the subnormal, and the seriously handicapped. Support for paediatric euthanasia, for example, is considerable. Enthusiasm for these grim ends is not an aberration in the euthanasia movement; it merely spells out the real logic of support for voluntary euthanasia. Once you begin to behave as if you have good reason to kill people when you judge they no longer have worthwhile lives, then why limit killing to those who ask for death? When you think that some human beings are lacking in all dignity, why should you respect their lives when you have power over them? As Chesterton perceptively observed many years ago: 'Some are proposing what is called euthanasia; at present only a proposal for killing those who are a nuisance to themselves; but soon to be applied to those who are a nuisance to other people.'

The political liberal may persist in arguing that a man should be at liberty to satisfy any of his desires, providing that in doing so he causes no harm to his fellow human beings. Such liberty, it is claimed, is the precondition for, if not the substance of, autonomy and self-determination.

I confine myself to three observations on this claim.

The first is that voluntary euthanasia is not an exercise of autonomy or self-determination. The habit of thinking that it is is much encouraged by the deceptive expression 'assisted suicide'. But voluntary euthanasia is never a case of someone killing himself, but always a case of someone being killed by another person. And when we are asked to legalise it we are being asked to accept that killing of one private citizen by another may be justified on the grounds that a human being's life lacks value, is not worthwhile.

The second observation is that we do not value political freedom or liberty as a freedom to satisfy whatever desires people just *happen* to have. Our sense of the value of freedom arises from our sense of the importance of developing in such a way that we come to be able to distinguish between intrinsically worthwhile desires and worthless desires.

'Satisfaction of some desires makes for human fulfilment, satisfaction of others for human misery. In so far as human beings are able to identify with intrinsically worthwhile desires and to engage in stable commitments and projects in pursuit of the realisation of those desires, they show themselves to be human beings who have achieved autonomy or a state of genuine self-determination. Political freedom is valuable in providing opportunity for the exercise of autonomy in this sense.

'But this ideal development could not have been achieved without the existence of institutions (such as the family, the school, the university) which impose constraints conducive to the formation of genuinely autonomous persons. So the existence of autonomous agents *presupposes* constraints.... Now, clearly, one of the institutions whose constraints are conducive to the formation of the autonomous individual is the criminal law. Knowledge that one lives in a society governed by norms of justice provides a sense of elementary security, without which there cannot be that sense of belonging to a community which is so conducive to nurturing autonomy. It would be radically destructive of this arrangement if it became lawful to kill a person because "he did not have a worthwhile life".... So a true sense of the requirements for autonomy ought to lead us to reject the legalisation of voluntary euthanasia.' [6]

My third comment on the political liberal's plea that a man should be at liberty to satisfy any of his desires providing that in doing so he causes no harm to his fellow human beings, is that satisfaction of the desire to be killed by a doctor does incalculable harm to the doctor and thereby to the practice of medicine. The harm done to the doctor is that his character is deeply corrupted by his euthanasiast decision.

Why should this be so? The practice of medicine necessarily exposes doctors to horrible things and obliges them to make tragic decisions. Why should the addition of euthanasia to a doctor's repertoire make such a difference to men who are in any case obliged, for instance, to balance the likely death resulting from a treatment against the pain and trouble caused by withholding it? The explanation lies in a distinction of quite fundamental importance for understanding the moral life, a distinction which, however, is widely regarded by utilitarian philosophers as opaque. The distinction is between what I intentionally bring about and what I bring about as the foreseen consequence of what I intend. In general what I intend to do is precisely what I choose to bring about, either as the end I am aiming to achieve or as the means necessary to secure my end. Choice is of quite central importance in our lives. One's choice of ends and of means manifests the dispositions of one's will - the directions in which one is inclined to move in life. And in making choices and commitments one shapes and establishes dispositions, as well as giving expression to established dispositions. The dispositions that we form in ourselves through our choices may be dispositions of a kind which better enable us to flourish as human beings in the way we are meant to flourish, or they may be destructive of our capacities to flourish, serving to head us in false directions in life. An example. In response to the invitation of the organisers of this Conference I chose to give this talk. In order to give the talk I chose to prepare a text. My chosen end is making some contribution to your enlightenment. My chosen means is preparing and delivering the text. Both choices serve to give expression to, and perhaps even to deepen, a commitment to convey certain important truths, of which I think I have some understanding.

But among the foreseeable consequences of my choices - all too foreseeable, I fear - are that I will induce bafflement in some, boredom in others, and others will go away with misunderstandings I did not seek to convey. Now of course I am not committed to achieving any of these results, nor others, such as tiredness in myself. They are results I will foreseeably produce, but they are not results which could count as evidence of what I *want* to achieve. They do not show the fundamental dispositions of my will, or shape those dispositions in desirable or undesirable directions.

That does not mean, of course, that the boredom, bafflement and misunderstandings which arise in consequence of what I say are outside my control. Perhaps if I performed better some of these consequences could be avoided. But let us suppose that I am speaking as well as I can speak about matters like this, but boredom, bafflement and misunderstandings are nonetheless consequences, and foreseeable consequences, of what I am saying. It would still be the case that it would be within my control to avoid these consequences: by abandoning my choice to give the talk.

The example illustrates the general distinction I have been seeking to explain. Some of the things I bring about in acting I *intend* to bring about: they are the object of my choice. The objects of my choice are what in a full-blooded sense I *want*. What I want in this full-blooded sense both manifests and shapes those fundamental dispositions which constitute my character, a character which either enables me to flourish as a human being or disables me.

Other things I bring about in acting, like most of the foreseeable consequences of what I do, I do not want in the same sense that I want my chosen end and means. The fact that I bring such consequences about (boredom, bafflement and misunderstandings) does not serve to shape my dispositions of character. There is, however, a sense in which it may be said that I am *willing* they should come about: for I am aware that I could *avoid* bringing them about if I were to abandon my chosen end and means.

The distinction between what I intend to bring about and what I am willing to allow to happen (as a consequence of actions which I have good reason to do) is of very great importance in medical ethics. Sometimes death is a consequence of what one does, not in the sense that it is the object of one's choice in a way which would make one into a killer, but rather in the sense that one is willing that death should occur because one had good reason to do, or refrain from doing, something in consequence of which death is foreseeable.

The doctor who carries out euthanasia makes the death of the patient the object of his choice, at least in the sense that the death of the patient is the chosen means to end a life believed no longer worthwhile. But in making the death of the patient the object of his choice the doctor profoundly shapes - and corrupts - his own dispositions. He makes his own the belief that some human beings lack dignity so that their lives may be disposed of without considerations of justice, and he acts on that belief: he becomes, morally speaking, a murderer.

There is by now a substantial body of historical scholarship showing the connection between the practical acceptance, by many German doctors in the 1920s, of the belief that there are lives without value, devoid of dignity, no longer worthwhile, which issued in the practice of voluntary and non-voluntary euthanasia, and the subsequent complicity of many members of the medical profession in the more extensively murderous practices of the Nazis.[7] The connection is simply that many of those doctors had already made themselves murderers: there was little or nothing in their beliefs, attitudes and character to stand in the way of such complicity. It is only an insane *hubris*, which feeds on illusions of moral respectability, that could induce us to believe that our own doctors could not be corrupted as those German doctors of the 1920s and 1930s were.

The loss of a sense of the dignity of every human being is deeply corrupting to the practice of medicine and nursing. Human beings have a claim on skilled care just because they are human beings and not because of status or achievement. Nor do they lose that claim because of debility or degeneration.

Propaganda for euthanasia, when it adopts the rhetoric of political liberalism, when it speaks of everyone being entitled to the satisfaction of his desires in the name of autonomy, is symptomatic of the predicament of our age and the predicament of medicine in our age. The rhetoric of political liberalism is the voice of a culture of atomic individuals. The atomic, isolated individual - the condition of increasing numbers in our society - experiences degeneration and increasing dependency as tantamount to a radical loss of dignity. People in that state of mind do not think it possible they could be cherished and esteemed whatever their condition.

Human beings who believe that their dignity is essentially tied up with a particular quality of life need, when they ask for euthanasia, to be cared for in ways which affirm their dignity and humanity, a dignity and humanity recognised in the face of debility, decay and dependency. In this way some of them may be restored to a recognition of that truth about themselves from which they have been too long alienated: the deepest source of their dignity lies not in an ultimately fragile capacity for independence, but in the humanity they share with all other men and women. This dignity we receive in being created, so it rests not on our fragile capacity for independence but on a radical and unbreakable dependence on the one who created us. Our human task is to cherish each other in the consciousness of that common dependence and our common dignity.

Because we live in a society which is characterised by profound moral differences, medicine as an instituiton is no longer sustained by a shared understanding of its proper and limited goal. In the consequent confusion many doctors are tempted to see themselves merely as possessors of a range of technical skills to be placed at the disposal of patients for the satisfaction of whatever desires patients want satisfied.

In this perspective euthanasia can become the final technical 'fix' in the doctor's repertoire. Confronted by the demand for euthanasia from patients who are experiencing a profound loss of self-esteem, the doctor who is willing to offer it is in effect saying: What you *now* think is correct; your lives are worthless, useless, without dignity. Better to end them.

But this is not the truth about human beings. Even *in extremis*, in dependency and degeneration, they may yet glimpse the truth about their own dignity which has been hidden from them for the whole of their lives. Dying can be a time of truth if we accept, rather than revolt against, the dependency that goes with it. Medicine should not aspire to rob us of this opportunity by offering killing as its final technical 'fix' - a killing which is premised on a radical rejection of human dignity.[8]

1 See chapter 3

2 A lawyer at the Conference was heard (by another lawyer) to
dismiss the belief I here express that there can be intentional killing
by omission. There is no doubt that in English law there can be
murder by a course of omissions intended to cause death. In the text
of the paper I speak of such omissions as chosen 'precisely with a
view to bringing about death'. This in fact represents too narrow an
understanding of what is required in law for murder by omission, as
will be evident from the following direction approved by the Court
of Criminal Appeal in *R v Gibbins and Proctor* (1918) 13 Cr. App.
R.134 at 137-8:

> ...if you think that one or other of these prisoners wilfully and
> intentionally withheld food from that child so as to cause her to
> weaken and to cause her grievous bodily injury, as the result of
> which she died, it is not necessary for you to find that she
> intended or he intended to kill the child then and there. It is
> enough if you find that he or she *intended to set up such a set of
> facts by withholding food or anything as would in the ordinary
> course of nature lead gradually but surely to her death* (emphasis
> added).

The Court in *Gibbins and Proctor* was aware of many earlier
directions to like effect, and specifically approved that given in *R. v
Bubb and Hook* (1850) 10 Cox C.C. 455 at 459. The concept of
murder by omission is fully confirmed by the Infanticide Act 1938,
s.1 (1), and the Homicide Act 1957, s.2 (1). (I am indebted for the
foregoing to an unpublished paper by Professor J.M. Finnis, 'Murder
and Paediatric "Holding Operations"'.)

The applicability of the direction in *Gibbins and Proctor* in *Regina v
Arthur* (1981) was strangely and conspicuously overlooked by the
judge in that case. But it will be recalled that in a written answer to
a question about that case the then Attorney General, Sir Michael
Havers, concluded:

> I am mindful of the desire of many people to understand clearly
> what the legal position is in relation to cases such as gave rise to
> the prosecution of Dr Arthur. I therefore say that I am satisfied
> that the law relating to murder and attempted murder is the same
> now as it was before the trial; that it is the same irrespective of
> the age of the victim; that it is the same irrespective of the
> wishes of the parents or any other person having a duty of care to

the victim. I am also satisfied that *a person who has duty of care may be guilty of murder or attempted murder by omitting to fulfil that duty, as much as by committing any positive act.* (Hansard, 9 March 1982, col.349; emphasis added.)

The most noteworthy oversight in the Report of the British Medical Association's Working Party on *Euthanasia* (London, BMA 1988) is its failure to recognise that an intention to kill may be accomplished by planned omissions. Paragraph 92 of the Report understands decisions to terminate someone's life as essentially involving 'an act or intervention which causes death'. The Report's failure to recognise 'intentional killing by omission' is directly connected with what, in my view, is the clearly euthanasiast recommendation (in paragraph 134) on what to do about babies with severe defects who may succeed in being 'lingering survivors': 'Hydration should be provided and the patient should not be deprived of the normal cuddling that expresses a fundamental human concern'; in other words, it is acceptable to deprive the child of normal nutrition in order to ensure that it does not succeed in being a 'lingering survivor'. Paragraph 134 reveals a glaring Achilles' heel in the BMA Committee's supposed opposition to euthanasia. It is clear from paragraphs 172-175 that some of the decisions taken in some UK paediatric units are euthanasiast: but this fact about present practice is not acknowledged by the Working Party. For a fuller discussion of these matters see the Linacre Centre Working Party Report *Euthanasia and Clinical Practice: trends, principles and alternatives* (London, The Linacre Centre, 1982), especially pp. 5-10, 32-34, 50-53, 55-61, 63-66.

3 The Chairman of the Voluntary Euthanasia Society has sought to argue that to describe voluntary euthanasia as killing betrays a blindness to conceptual distinctions: the distinction is as obvious, she says, as the distinction between rape and 'making love'. (See Jean Davies 'Raping and making love are different concepts: so are killing and voluntary euthanasia' in *Journal of Medical Ethics* 14 (1988), 148-149). 'Making love' is itself a morally ambiguous euphemism, often employed in our society to describe sexual intercourse whether in a marital relationship, in an adulterous relationship, or in fornication. Rape is defined as 'unlawful sexual intercourse with a woman without her consent'. It is distinguished from marital intercourse, adulterous intercourse and fornication by the absence of consent. But what it has in common with them is its being an act of sexual intercourse. Similarly, judicial execution of a man for a capital offence and euthanasia have in common that they are acts of killing. The question of which of the acts, if any, is justified is not

settled by the description of them as 'killing', any more than a similar question is settled about acts which can all be described as 'sexual intercourse' by the mere use of that description (nor, for that matter, would it be settled if all the acts were euphemistically describable as 'making love').

4   See Luke Gormally, 'A Non-Utilitarian Case against Voluntary Euthanasia', in A.B. Downing and B. Smoker, eds, *Voluntary Euthanasia,* London, Peter Owen, 1986, 72-95.

5   For a position of the kind referred to see the letter from Mrs Jean Davies, Chairman of the Voluntary Euthanasia Society, in *IME Bulletin* No 48 (March 1989), p.2; see my reply in *IME Bulletin* No. 50 (May 1989), p.2.

6   In these two paragraphs I repeat something of what I say at pp. 84-85 of the article cited in note 4.

7   These developments were first chronicled by Dr Leo Alexander in the article reprinted as Chapter 2, above.

8   After my criticism of the BMA Report in note 1 above, I should like to acknowledge that the Report contains paragraphs which finely express the profound inappropriateness of euthanasia as a solution to the human predicament of *adult* patients who are dying in pain and distress. Particularly notable among these paragraphs is 146:

> It is precisely because human life has depths, and a value that may take fresh and unexpected form, even up until the moment of death, that it must not be cut short. This commitment to the preservation of life must be tempered with a sensitivity to the wishes and experiences of the dying patient. That sensitivity, indeed reverence, may be blunted, as medical sensitivities so often are, when there is an accepted 'treatment' to be offered rather than an ethically demanding situation to be confronted. Opting for a 'treatment' - voluntary euthanasia - which can be administered given certain indications precipitates the danger of substituting a technique (which draws on professional skill) for a human response in the midst of a deeply human experience which, above all, requires us to draw on our full character as human beings. This implies that a reverence for persons, and for the way that we ought to relate to persons in need and for the kinds of persons we want our doctors to be, tells *against* rather than *for* euthanasia.

5

Dying to Die?

E. David Cook

Woody Allen inevitably has a memorable line: 'I'm not afraid of dying. I just don't want to be there when it happens'. We all know how he feels, for death in our culture has not simply become a great unmentionable, it has become feared. But that fear is not quite manifested by everyone.

In a recent television programme on BBC with Kilroy Silk, the bias of the programme and the attitudes of people were clearly shown. It was a programme based on the theme of euthanasia. It began with a lady recounting how she had helped her friend to die. The friend was bedridden, and had saved up enough pills to take her own life. She didn't want to die alone, so asked her friend to be with her. Her friend agreed and held her hand as she had taken the pills and tried to die. The friend noticed after a while that she was not dead. Kilroy asked what she did then. 'I held a plastic bag over her head to make sure she did die.' 'What happened then?' was his next question. 'I went home and she was found the next day by her cleaner. Then I was arrested and sent to prison.' The audience showed all too clearly their disapproval of such a callous act. The callous act of sending an old lady to prison for killing with kindness. That was the signal for a series of horror stories of helping relatives to die and of the medical profession striving to keep people alive long after the relatives wanted and, allegedly, against the patient's will.

The audience selected to appear was interesting. There were spouses, parents and relatives of those who had 'benefited' from euthanasia or 'suffered' at the hands of the medical profession. There were Voluntary Euthanasia Society activists and clergy supporters. There were a number of people suffering from severe handicap or fatal illnesses, including some AIDS patients. There was a small band of those opposed to the practice of euthanasia.

The points at issue in the programme reinforced a general trend in society towards the practice of euthanasia and an increasing pressure on medical and nursing staff and within Parliament for a change in legislation to permit euthanasia under certain circumstances. The arguments took the following forms. Friends and families argued that we treat animals better than human beings. We are quite happy - indeed feel it to be our moral responsibility and an act of compassion - to put an animal down. Why should we treat human beings with less love and care? This is especially the case with those we love. If we love them, then we will refuse to allow them to suffer - and put them out of their misery. Behind this argument based on compassion there is the recognition that self-interest is not totally absent. The distress that families and relatives feel, the demands made on them in terms of visits, care and responsibility and the strain of watching their loved ones losing their dignity and slowly and painfully deteriorating and dying are all factors in the pressure to help people to die.

The person who is ill (especially if the disease is severely handicapping and fatal) argues that the loss of dignity in terms of growing dependence and loss of functions and capacities, the quality of life in prospect, and the basic right of autonomy to choose what should happen to us and our bodies, all clearly point to the right to euthanasia. This was highlighted for me by two cases. The first was from those suffering from AIDS. They knew only too well what kind of living and death faced them. They were already aware that their mental functioning would be, and perhaps even now was, affected so that rational choice would be impossible. They saw themselves as a risk to others - to families, friends and loved ones. They did not wish to make a mistake and leave themselves as 'vegetables' requiring even more costly care than they were beginning and would continue to need. As they saw it, their desire to die with dignity was matched by society's desire to protect itself, and the medical profession should thus act responsibly and end their lives. The other example was of an attractive lady who worked in the City of London. She had had a colostomy and now had developed major stomach and abdominal cancer. She had discussed with her relatives her plans and had collected a supply of drugs to enable her to end her own life. In response to my question about how and when she would decide that the time had come to take her own life, she replied that it was when she was no longer able to put on her make-up herself. That for her was the dividing line between dignity and indignity. She claimed that she would much prefer the Dutch situation and be able to take advantage of a euthanasia clinic, where her death would be medically organized and supervised. It was her body, and she had the right to do with it whatever she wished.

Behind the AIDS sufferers' argument lies the idea that society and the community have the right to defend themselves and to protect the rest of their members from risks caused by some members. In a way it is an extension of the punishment model. If someone breaks the law, then society must act, punish and defend itself. If someone is a risk he must be removed. If that person himself is willing and demands to be removed from the scene once and for all and that person is a risk, a serious cost, and will offer no benefit to the rest of us, then he should be helped to die.

This kind of argument finds its focus in the basis of the Voluntary Euthanasia Society. Its members have long argued that we all have a right to die and a right to be killed, if we so desire. The rights of the individual are paramount and must be safeguarded and fulfilled. Medicine exists for the sake of and benefit of us all. It is to be our servant and not its own master. It must do what we wish it to do. In a civilized society, people have the right to death with dignity and the medical profession needs to recognize that the choice of when death should come must belong to the patient and his or her relatives. Compassion, human rights and common sense all agree that people should not be kept alive against their will.

There is support for such a position within the ranks of the church. Some clergy argue that we do have a right to die with dignity, and this is part of what it means to be made in the image of God. They are more concerned, though, with the practice of compassion. Love does not allow people to suffer. Love acts to relieve pain and distress. Love takes life and does not preserve it needlessly or pointlessly. Love kills if the other asks and if love is thus best served.

It will do us no service whatsoever to underestimate the strength of feeling and the widespread support for the positions here underlined. There is a shift within our culture to support euthanasia, and the battle will be fought in Parliament ere too long. It behoves Christians to prepare for that battle and to offer both a critical response to the arguments and presuppositions behind the pro-euthanasia position, as well as to present as winsomely and cogently as possible an alternative - if we believe that God has a better way for human beings to live and die. But whatever arguments are mounted, they must be realistic and based on grounds that will appeal to society at large. Our own Christian proclamation must be set alongside an appeal to the hearts and minds of secular society.

Public Opinion

Newsweek magazine in an article on March 14 1988 entitled 'A Right To Die?' argued that on an average of six times a day a doctor in Holland practises 'active' euthanasia: intentionally administering a lethal drug to a terminally ill patient who has asked to be relieved of suffering. *Newsweek* went on: 'Recent polls in Britain show that 72 percent of British subjects favour euthanasia in some circumstances. An astonishing 76 percent of respondents to a poll taken last year in France said they would like the law changed to decriminalize mercy killings' (*Newsweek* March 14 1988, p. 46).

There seems little doubt that the tide is flowing in the pro-euthanasia direction, but what arguments underlie such a position? One key theme is that of a 'licence to kill' under certain circumstances. Such people look to the law to frame adequate legislation to permit the taking of life. This raises the issue of what kinds of laws we shall have and how these laws impact the medical and nursing professions. What is clear from our experience of the abortion law is that what begins as allowing certain actions in limited circumstances soon degenerates into an expectation, and what is then seen as a requirement, to act under any circumstances. The medical and nursing professions need to be more aware of the likely impact of legal changes on their professional standards and practices.

The law is one form of expression of the kind of society we are and the values we seek to uphold by enshrining them in law. Laws set limits to what we will and will not tolerate in our society. Our laws are such that they sometimes do grant a licence to kill.

1. War

In warfare, defence of others and self-defence, there is for people a right to kill. Of course, this is not an absolute, unmitigated right, but it is an expression of the idea that homicide is permissible and justifiable under certain circumstances. There is a good reason to kill people. It is often the only apparent means of preventing them from killing others.

2. Capital Punishment

The yearly debate on the theme of capital punishment underlines the gap between public opinion, which is solidly in favour of capital punishment, and the House of Commons' steadfast refusal to return to what it regards as barbaric - and open to mistake. Capital punishment is in essence a licence to kill. The taking of a life in those circumstances is seen as the appropriate response to the taking of other people's lives. It is a way of restoring the balance of the scales of justice. It both limits the harm and killing done to others and shows the seriousness of the initial act of murder. The killer is seen as one who has set him or herself outside the law. His life is thus legitimately forfeit.

3. Abortion

Neither in war nor in capital punishment is the killing envisaged as indiscriminate. The licence to kill is strictly limited. So also in the case of abortion. Abortions are permitted in law under certain specifiable circumstances: before twenty eight weeks, if the health of the mother is at risk, or if the degree of abnormality is considered severe, and so on. Thus this licence to kill is set within limits. Part of the nature of such legislation is that the very process of setting limits seems itself such a reasonable exercise that the limits themselves become 'reasonable' to us. It thus becomes all the more difficult to refuse and reject the whole procedure. Following J. Rawls we need to note the important difference between the setting up of standards and the arguments which are based on and assume those standards. We may easily confuse arguments about which set of standards to adopt with those concerning whether we ought to allow any standards at all to be set in matters of life and death.

For those whose response to war, capital punishment, abortion and euthanasia is part of a seamless robe of rejection, the taking of life is absolutely forbidden. Thus for the conscientious objector, the pacifist, the anti-hanging lobby and the pro-life groups there are clear moral and religious objections to the taking of life. For them there is no licence to kill. In contrast, there are those who disagree and argue that the taking of life is permissible and justifiable under certain circumstances. What justification, then, is usually offered for the act of killing? There are two broad forms of argument presented.

Justifying Killing
1. For the good of the patient.
It is held that at certain times it is in the best interest of the patient to end his or her life. In some cases of the severely malformed, the terminally ill, the senile and the unwanted or deformed foetus, it is for their own good that they should die. There are at least three separate elements to this kind of argument. The first deals with those cases where the patient has requested death. They have asked to die. This rests on the notion of human autonomy and freedom. We have the right to decide our own fate. We ought to be masters and mistresses of our own bodies. We have the right to die and the right to be

killed. Patients in this case have asked to die. They have
given permission to be killed.

The second line of argument is that this kind of killing
spares further suffering. It is a means of drawing a line
beyond which we will not allow people to suffer, it
recognises that there are limits to what we expect others
to endure and which we will allow people to tolerate. This
holds both for those who have requested death and for
those who are unable to make such a request. It rests on
the assumption that if they were able to articulate, then
they would seek to die. Death is a better alternative than
a life of suffering. The aim in all this is the alleviation of
suffering. Animals are relieved from their pain and so must
human beings be. Compassion and love mean the
alleviation of pain and suffering.

A third strand of argument is that the quality of life of
the individual in these cases is that of a life not worth
living. This is not simply an account of the current
situation, but makes a calculation of the prognosis, future
expectations and hope. The quality of life present and to
come seems so poor that such life is not worth living.

2. For the good of others.
The second main base in support of some limited licence to
kill is on the grounds of the good it will lead to for others.
The killing of the severely malformed child, the terminally
ill, the senile and the foetus are to be permitted if it will
lead to the benefit of others. There are many aspects to
the argument, but three form the usual core of this
position.

Such killing will spare the suffering of those close to and
involved with the patient. In particular, it will bring much
needed relief to relatives and families. They are the ones
who suffer directly both in the effect on their lives,– the
disruption, the demands and responsibilities,– as well as

in the watching, often helplessly, of the suffering and agony of a loved one. For their sake, it may be right to take the life of another.

A second strand is in economic terms. The cost of keeping people alive is too great. The handicapped, the senile, the terminally ill make excessive demands on pointless treatment. The clearest current example arises in the debate over treating AIDS patients. At the present state of medical science, we know that there is no cure for AIDS. Those who develop the full-blown syndrome will die. Nothing we can do can prevent that, even if some forms of treatment may slow down the process. Given that there is no cure, why waste good money on helping those who cannot be helped? Given the crying needs in all manner of health areas where people can be helped and their life improved, it makes no sense at all to spend money on AIDS patients when the money could be spent in a worthwhile and constructive way for the benefit of others.

Part of this is also an argument about the wisdom of spending money on extraordinary measures which cost massive amounts, when the sums involved could be easily redirected to hosts of other cheaper branches of medical care. Justice requires that the many be treated rather than the few. At a time of economic cutbacks in the National Health Service, the never-ending set of demands for money requires hard economic decisions to be made. There is little cost benefit to be gained in keeping alive those whose lives are limited and painful and who have no genuine possibility of improvement and cure. There are much more profitable ways of allocating our limited resources for the benefit of others.

There is a third subset of the argument which is not afraid to state that for the sake of the majority it may be necessary and profitable to rid ourselves and our society of what is a risk, offensive, unacceptable and makes no contribution to the well-being of our society. It is all too evident that some of the hysteria we have witnessed in people's reactions to AIDS victims could all too easily lead to the compulsory removal of such victims from society. The move to the concentration camp can all too readily end up with a 'final' solution for the benefit of the greatest number.

For the good of the patient - Response
There does seem an oddity in suggesting that death is for the good of the person involved. Does this actually make sense? Can it be better to kill someone than to let them live? The question is, in what sense 'better'? How can I know that it will benefit them, and how can they know that? How can I ask them afterwards? 'Are you really happier dead than living the way you did?' This becomes even more complicated in the case of those who are unable to decide for themselves and who are unable to express a view of their quality of life. Yet there are obviously many who do claim the right to die, and who have given their consent to be killed.

There are all too many problems over what constitutes valid consent. Is the person who signed a living will at the age of twenty-five to be bound by that piece of paper when he or she is seventy-five? If that same seventy-five year old now signs another form how can we be sure that they have fully understood the issues, or whether they have had undue pressure from relatives, friends or even the medical and nursing staff? What happens if a large insurance policy is involved, or a hefty inheritance? The notion of consent is complex and fraught with difficulties. The request to die is beset with problems. How can one allow for a genuine change of mind, and freedom from undue and untoward pressure - especially of the subtle mental variety?

The acceptance of such a request rests on a particular view of human autonomy and freedom. It argues that we are free to do whatever we like with our own bodies and with our own life. Here there is a close parallel with suicide. The act of suicide or the demand to be killed - assisted suicide - is a rebellion against God as the Creator, Author, Sustainer, Preserver, and Lord of life. If life is indeed God's, then death is to be seen in the light of God. God created humanity. To be a creature is to be at the call and disposal of the Creator. This is our human situation. Life and death are not ultimately in our own hands, but rest in the hands of God. If he is the Sovereign One then that sovereignty must include ultimate control over life and death. God is the giver and taker of life. To imagine that our lives are our own to do with as we please is to rebel against God and to seek to usurp his place and role.

Suicide is a rebellion against God, not only because it tries to take the place of God and to exercise his rights, but also because it fails to recognise that life as a gift from God brings certain responsibilities. When human beings are given life it is in the form of a loan. Our life does not belong to us. We cannot do whatever we like with our lives. The created person is a steward of God. That means that we are answerable to God for the whole of creation and for how we use and care for the created order. This must also mean that we are stewards of God with respect to our lives. We are answerable and accountable to God for life itself and how we use it in our service for him. We are not free to return the loan of life whenever we feel like it. It has a term fixed by God. He calls us to account in his own good time, and we are to look to him to do his will in humble obedience.

Here the medical profession has to admit that its zeal and refusal to come to terms with its fallibility has meant that some patients have been artificially kept alive long after it was appropriate. Death is not to be feared at all costs. The attitude to death of patient and doctor alike lies at the heart of these dilemmas and needs further reflection.

But the notion of freedom is part of a societal framework of thought. In the name of individual freedom, then, all things seem to be demanded and required. But freedom makes little or no sense without some idea of boundaries and limits. Freedom is never an absolute in a society, so we need to stop pretending that it is. Our society does allow people the freedom to die within certain limits, but that is not the same as the freedom to be killed. A suicide takes life by his or her own hand. Euthanasia is not an isolated activity. It involves other people. Here lies the root of key limitations of freedom. My freedom cannot infringe on and remove the freedom of someone else. In demanding euthanasia, I am demanding the doctor surrender his or her freedom to serve my need. This removes the autonomy from another. It is hard to see that a sound argument based on autonomy and freedom would end up removing autonomy and freedom.

Equally the notion of rights which lies at the root of much of the euthanasia debate must be more critically examined. Christians need to be more careful in embracing talk of rights, and need to ask whether such talk is biblical. The language of rights is part of a secular Western humanistic philosophy. Whence do such rights arise? Are they natural rights found in the nature of the world and in human nature? Are they legal rights enshrined in legal codes and thus simply a human creation? Are they part of what it means to be created in the image of God, and if so which rights do we have as creatures? Is it true that we can hold some truths to be self-evident - that all men are created equal and are endowed with certain inalienable rights and among these are life, liberty and the pursuit of happiness? Does the right to die and be killed form a part of those rights? For whom are such rights, and when? Talk of the right to die is an oddity, for death is an inevitable process. How then may I have a right to do what I shall necessarily experience?

Talk of rights implies responsibilities. The right to die implies the responsibility of someone to take life. It is interesting to speculate on a society which stressed responsibilities rather than rights and what difference that might make. Again we are inevitably cast into a situation of conflicting rights. Can I have the right to live and the right to die at the same time? If I have the right to die, does someone else have the right to refuse to kill me, and how is that conflict to be resolved? If I have a right to die, does society have the right to keep me alive for its good? Bland talk of human rights covers a host of confusions which require careful and thorough treatment. 'Rights' talk is all too often sloganising rather than argumentation.

The second line of argument was based on the need to spare further suffering. Concern to alleviate pain and suffering is one mark of genuine love. But this must not lead to glib or simplistic responses to the problem of pain. To kill someone and thus 'put them out of their misery' assumes that there is no other way to control or alleviate pain, and that pain has no point. Both may be queried. The hospice movement is rightly famed for its care of the dying, and its work on pain control. The picture of someone dying in agony should not be the case in reality. It is all too often based on anecdotal evidence of long ago. It is up to the medical profession to be more aware of the advances in this aspect of medical practice, and to refuse to allow their patients pain-filled lives.

Of course, there was a time when such pain control meant that the patient lost dignity and became dependent on the drugs and reduced to a zombie. Again this misapplication of drugs can be remedied by the careful, personally tailored dosage of drugs, which achieves a balance between pain control and consciousness. It is remarkable what can be done in this area with adequate time and expertise.

The more difficult rebuttal of the argument based on sparing suffering is to suggest that pain may have a point or purpose. Part of our unease is that so often pain is obviously destructive in its effects on all concerned. Christians can be simplistic and downright dishonest in stating their case here, but bad expressions of the point do not undermine the validity of the view.

Pain often acts as a warning and enables people to realise that something is wrong and to seek help to put things right. But it may also have a deeper point in the life of the individual. Many attest to discovering their true humanity, something basic about themselves, or a closer relationship with others and with God as a result of painful experience. Suffering and pain are not easy to understand, but that does not make them totally meaningless. We can catch glimpses of the positive qualities suffering can elicit in ourselves and in others. This is not so much to give reasons for all suffering, but rather to deny that there are no reasons to be found. The suffering and death of Christ showed where suffering can lead.

Behind the debate over sparing suffering lies our view of the context and meaning of life. How we react to difficult and painful situations reveals our very basic beliefs. The story of Job gives an account of a man trying to make sense out of personal suffering both physical and mental. Job never receives a direct answer to his problem of why he suffers. But by the end of the book he is given a vision of God. At this point all Job's questions pale into insignificance, compared to the overwhelming sense of the presence of God. The sight of God puts not only life and death, but also pain and suffering, in a new context.

The reality is that most of us do not see our pain in the light of God, but rather in terms of the absence of pleasure. Our society is in the business of being happy. In a way we are all hedonists, eating, drinking and being merry. We expect to be pain-free, and modern medicine has reinforced that expectation. The problem of over-prescribing is not only a comment on hard-pressed general practice but on the demanding nature of patients. We all expect the doctor to take away our pain. Indeed, our opening gambit in the surgery is 'Please give me something for my....' The impressive range of painkillers available both over the chemist's counter and on prescription means that we expect to have no pain. The growing dimensions of the drug abuse scene and increasing dependence on tranquillizers should warn us of some of the dangers of our view of pleasure.

This is not to argue for stoicism, nor a withholding of needed drugs, but a greater care in light of the dangers of drug abuse and dependency. The problem for the hard-pressed medic is knowing when and how to intervene. If it is argued that there are limits to what people can tolerate in terms of pain we move immediately into a difficult realm. How much pain can each of us tolerate, and is there a norm, or endless variation? Part of the problem of over-prescription was a failure to appreciate different levels of need and sensitivity to drugs.

It is also hard to decide when one has reached the limits of tolerance. If I cry out in my pain and tell a doctor that I cannot take any more, am I to be taken so seriously that I am put out of my misery, even though I might change my mind after another injection or when the spasm of pain went? Does someone else have the right or the ability to know when the limit has been reached? Pain and its relief seem to be subjective and subject to widely differing levels of tolerance. There seems to be no blanket strategy which can be applied to all regardless, but rather a need for individualised pain care - and that inevitably means more and better trained staff.

The basic motive in so much of traditional medicine has been that of compassion. It is in the name of compassion that we are being called on to practise euthanasia. Is compassion a kindness that kills? Are there limits to what we should do in the name of compassion? Does compassion always mean acceding to the demands and requests of a patient? Should a doctor never say 'No'? Is compassion doing what someone wants? Part of the point behind these questions is a concern that love and compassion are being used in such a widely-defined way that they lose not only their traditional content but any genuine meaning. The issue is what it means to love someone properly. That may mean helping them cope with their life as it is, rather than helping them exit from it.

Part of this may be helping people consider more carefully whether their life is worth living. The question of the 'quality of life' is often a basic theme in the pro-euthanasia case. This reminds us of the difficulty of knowing whether or not a life is worth living now, and even more problematically in the future. To compare two things requires some agreed criteria which make the comparison genuine. It is far from clear how we can compare a situation of living with one of the absence of sensation and life itself. The particular fear here is of those who are used to a particular standard of living making judgements about and for those whose normal quality of life is very different from that of the majority of other people. The notion of what is fitting and appropriate seems helpful here. What is appropriate and fitting for a neo-nate is not fitting for a young adult. The expectations of the elderly must be very different from those of the middle-aged, and we need to deliver ourselves from unhelpful and unrealistic comparisons of unlike with unlike. That the quality of life now available is much less than we may have enjoyed when we were twenty years younger, even if the life of the handicapped is fundamentally different from able-bodied living, does not mean that life is not worth living and has less value to those who have nothing *else* to live - and who may *know* nothing else. It does seem that the proper response to the question of whether or not life is worth living must involve some clear picture of the individual and his or her attitudes and beliefs. One attempt to express what the Americans call a 'living will' embodies a picture of the life which one person may regard as not worth living, or rather the circumstances which might point to a negative judgement about the quality of life involved.

'I wish to live a full and long life, but not at all costs. If my death is near and cannot be avoided, and if I have lost the ability to interrelate with others and have no reasonable chance of regaining this ability, or if my suffering is intense and irreversible, I do not want to have my life prolonged. I would then ask not to be subjected to surgery or resuscitation. Nor would I then wish to have life support from mechanical ventilators, intensive-care services, or other life-prolonging procedures, including the administration of antibiotics and blood products. I would wish, rather, to have care which gives comfort and support, which facilitates my interaction with others to the extent that this is possible, and which brings peace.'[1]

This quotation in its direct simplicity reveals a multitude of problems of definition and judgement. How and where different physicians would draw the lines is of the very

For the good of others - Response
This argument rests on the classic gambit of treating people as means to an end rather than ends in themselves. The basic premise undermines what has become a

---

[1] 'Personal Directions for Care at the End of Life'. Sissela Bok, New England Journal of Medicine 295, 1976, 369.

fundamental belief in Western society - that people are to be treated as ends in themselves and not as means to ends. Such manipulation destroys the dignity and intrinsic value and worth of the individual. It makes a person less than a person.

The nature of this argument is based on the principle of intrinsic value. It is often accompanied by an argument based on consequences. Once we allow treating people in this way and killing them for the sake of others, then we are all vulnerable. Today it may be the senile, the demented and the AIDS victim. Tomorrow it may be five-foot–seven Scotsmen and the normal, but socially, racially and politically unacceptable. This is a 'wedge' type of argument. If we give people an inch then they will take a mile. It warns us that the business of drawing lines depends on human nature. No matter how carefully we seek to limit what may be permitted, it seems that our human nature seeks to take advantage of whatever lines are drawn and to push both at and beyond the limits. Some argue that such slippery-slope arguments mean that we must be all the tighter in creating and maintaining the laws we make. How often are we able to put the clock back and to recover ground lost in the name of progress?

The idea that in taking life we are sparing the suffering of others, especially friends and relatives, assumes that we shall not merely replace the suffering of watching a loved one in pain with the guilt of having taken or having agreed to have taken the loved one's life. It also assumes that there can be no alleviation or improvement in terms of pain relief. But we have noted that pain can be controlled and that there may be a point even in the experience of pain.

The second part of the argument based on the good for others was that of economics. It is inevitable that we must make economic decisions, and they are often hard to make.

But there is always a distinction between economic and moral decision. When we have allocated resources purely on an economic basis, it is always possible to ask whether such a decision is right or wrong, good or bad. This is not just a question about the validity of the economics involved, but rather a question of morality. Morality and economics are independent of each other. If economic considerations are the sole basis for such a decision to end a person's life, then we are saying that people are merely economic units and we are in the inevitable business of trying to calculate their worth. Instinctively we feel that such a reduced view of human being is inadequate and unworthy, not just of the practice of medicine but as a basis for a society which calls itself civilised and modern. People are more, and more important than, economic factors.

To judge the worth of people in terms of their contribution to society may be pragmatic, but it hits at the very understanding of the nature of a person and his worth, value and dignity. We recognise that there are many who have made and will make little or no contribution to society, but that does not mean that we regard such folk as worthless and disposable. People's value does not depend on what they can contribute and produce. But that does raise for a secular society a key question about the value and worth of every individual.

To propound such a view does not mean that we are writing a blank cheque which may be endlessly drawn upon. Of course, resources in general and health resources in particular must be allocated sensibly. There is too much money being spent on extraordinary measures and esoteric medicine, and there does need to be some kind of adjudication about what is ordinary and what extraordinary medicine, what can reasonably be expected and demanded and what is essentially a luxury. Cost is a relevant factor, but not the sole or most important one.

and what is essentially a luxury. Cost is a relevant factor, but not the sole or most important one.

The third step in the argument was essentially an argument which leads to compulsory euthanasia. It is too easy to say that such a step evokes universal condemnation and to move on to the next point. Our history even in recent days suggests that we can be all too willing to condemn groups of people to death for the so-called benefit of the rest of us. It is not merely a question of the horrors of genocide and of the Nazi concentration camps, but let us not underestimate or forget them too readily. But we face a situation where people like AIDS sufferers are willing to recognize that they may present a risk to others and even to condone and ask for mercy-killing. This ought to concern us greatly. Human nature as it is is all too likely to welcome such a willingness and reasonable attitude and to seek to remove what is a risk and danger to others. But is this how human beings ought to behave and should our laws be framed so that this will be possible?

All the arguments based on the good for others ultimately reduce to a variation on the theme of the end justifying the means and the action. If good comes then we may do evil, seems to be the line of argument.

Presuppositions

J.O. Ormson said that we must all have a point by which to lever the world. He was suggesting that we all have various presuppositions which are the ground of our beliefs and values and which, because they are taken for granted, are often extremely hard to uncover and articulate. This is where the secular and the Christian set of values come into an inevitable conflict. In seeking an approach to the issue of euthanasia it is vital to consider the differing presuppositions and their significance in the debate. We shall offer a key set of areas for critical reflection and

analysis. These points lie at the very heart of the debate
and it is on this ground that the battle will be lost or won.

1. Moral Arguments

It is all too easy for Christians to characterize the pro–
euthanasia case as one simply based on consequences
rather than principles. While this is often the case it is not
necessarily so. The argument based on autonomy and
choice is in essence a principle–based argument, though it
often ends up in a consequencestressing form. The
problem is that the Christian often presents his or her
argument in a simplistic way as if he or she is not at all
interested in consequences. In reality the Christian ought
to be concerned with consequences as well as principles.
Results matter and are part of an holistic account of
morality.

But we are right to be concerned about an approach to
moral issues which stresses consequences and all too
often seems to reduce to consequences alone. The problem
is that we are unable to predict or control consequences.
Thus any and every morality which rests on consequences
alone is built on shifting sand and is less than an adequate
moral base. What happens may be very far from what I
intended or desired.

The basis of morality and how we make moral
judgements is at stake in the debate. Christians ought to
carry the day in terms of principles and consequences.

2. Autonomy and Freedom

For the secularist human beings are autonomous and free.
That gives us the right to do whatever we like with our
lives and our bodies. At times the stress on freedom
seems to imply that there are no limits at all to be set to
our freedom. This is a nonsense. To be part of a society is
to live in settings where we agree and accept limitations
on our autonomy. The law in particular seeks to structure

our agreement over what limits we may accept and tolerate.

The Christian goes a step further for freedom is replaced with a willing service of God. Our life is not our own but belongs to God and we are responsible and answerable to him for what we do and how we live and die. As stewards we are responsible to God for the use we make of all that we have been given. Responsibility is the basic theme of the Christian which makes us all our brothers' and sisters' keepers. Our human freedom is always limited by reference to God.

3. Rights
We have already seen something of the problem over human rights and their nature and origin. The current emphasis on rights seems often to exclude the correlative stress on responsibilities. But that is not the only difficulty with talk of rights. Such talk does not aid us in deciding in situations of conflict of rights, both for the individual and between individuals. We require another means of resolving conflict than 'rights' themselves. We need a much more critical and reflective account of the nature, origin, limits, responsibilities and conflicts involved in human rights, especially the right to die and the right to be killed.

4. Worth and Value
How much is a person worth? Some might want to see how much has been left behind in the will. Others might look at the contribution an individual makes to society, family or friends. Others again suggest that our worth really comes from our attitude towards ourselves. The slogan of the Black Power movement began with the clarion call, 'I am somebody'. How we see ourselves is the basis for some of worth and value. The real problem arises when people have nothing in the way of worldly goods, appear to make little or no contribution to society, seem to

be a drag on family and friends and have no sense of self-worth and value. Have such people then no worth?

The Christian affirms that the worth of a person stems from God. God created men and women, and that in itself gives us all worth. God made us in his image, so we have value because we are like God. He breathed his life into us, so our worth comes from the life of God in us. We were made to enjoy fellowship with God, so we have a purpose and a goal in life. Jesus Christ came, lived and died for us, so that again reveals our worth to the Father who sent him and to the One who lived and died for us. Worth and value lie for the Christian in God and our relationship with God.

One area that does need urgent attention is a discussion of dependency. The pro-euthanasia lobby seems to suggest that every form of dependency is degrading and dehumanizing. This is nonsense. If no-one is an island, then a necessary part of living in community is mutual interdependency. We need to recover a sense of what is appropriate and fitting, and that will include a proper sense of being dependent.

5. The Changing Perception of the Medical Profession
We live in a society where the role and perception of the medical and nursing professions is changing. The demand nature of our society pressurizes the medic into meeting our needs. Often a consultation begins with 'I want you to give me something for...'. If the doctor is nothing more than a need–meeter then it is little wonder that if I need to die I will expect the doctor to help kill me.

What is at stake is a vast shift from a traditional role of preserving life to becoming in some sense death controllers. In the pursuit of preserving life there have been many examples of over-zealous and inappropriate medicine. But that simply points to the need for the profession to exercise more care and to be better communicators.

Part of what will help is a more honest and careful analysis and unpacking of the difference between omission and commission. We need to be clearer about the distinction between killing and letting die. It is not enough to quote the maxim, 'Thou shalt not kill but need not strive officiously to keep alive.' Obviously some treatments will have fatal results. Sometimes the withholding of treatment will have fatal results. There does, however, seem an important distinction between rendering someone unconscious with the risk of killing him and rendering someone unconscious in order to kill him. The difference lies in the motive, and a fuller analysis of moral actions would deal not only with principles and consequences but also with motivation and its vital role.

In the final analysis the issue for the medical and nursing staff is one of practicalities. Does this treatment offer a reasonable chance of an appreciable duration of desirable life at an acceptable cost of suffering? The difficult elements in the question can only be answered in close liaison with the actual situations and medical judgments actually made.

6. The Law

The medical profession needs to consider very carefully the impact of legal changes on the profession and the public perception and expectations of that profession. Euthanasia legislation will challenge traditional views of doctors and their proper role. Before we encourage or accept such changes in law we should ensure that the case for such change is overwhelming and the necessity for adaptation secure. We should also expect that the results of such a move would produce a far superior situation. Unless both of these things are assured, we would do well to hesitate in making sweeping changes in our legislation.

7. Sanctity of Life

The sanctity of life can all too easily become a slogan in the euthanasia debate, but it does draw attention to a crucial need for doctors, patients, families and society to be clear about the value it places on life. Part of this is not just our attitude to the preservation of life, but also some account of our response to pain, suffering and death. We need to be more honest about what our actual beliefs are and the difference, if any, between Christians and non-Christians in their fear of death and dying. If we proclaim eternal life then what does this do in terms of how we live and how we die? Christians need to be more honest and consistent in their response to their own pain, suffering and death as well as to that of others.

The debate on euthanasia will only get more heated. The battle is on, and there is growing support for the practice and the idea. If we are to offer an alternative, then we need to counter the pro-euthanasia arguments and to expose the nature and content of the presuppositions which underlie such views. We must also present a Christian account which is both winsome and realistic. But both of these strategies will fail unless they are matched by behaviour which actually shows the difference. It is not enough for us to know the truth. We must incarnate our values in our living and dying. Doing that truth is all that we can do, and all that is required.

6

Euthanasia Reconsidered

Richard Higginson

Defining Terms

The word 'euthanasia' is a confusing one. It is important to try to dispel confusion at the start by clarifying what we are talking about.

There are various types of action, or refraining from action, which can be and have been described as euthanasia. The most typical appear to be as follows. First, there is the administration of drugs to patients with the express purpose of bringing about death. The drugs most likely to be used are barbiturates, morphine or depronal. Taken in sufficient quantities, they all have the effect of causing a deep depression of the respiratory system, thereby accelerating death. Curare, which paralyses the muscles, may also be used, though only after the patient has been rendered unconscious. This type of medical treatment is often known as 'active' or 'direct' euthanasia. (Type 1)

Second, there is the administration of drugs to patients with the purpose of reducing pain, which may as a side-effect bring forward the moment of death by depressing the respiratory system. This has sometimes been described as 'indirect' euthanasia. (Type 2)

Third, there is the act of discontinuing a particular form of treatment, because it is felt to be of no benefit to the patient. For example, a comatose patient might be taken off an artificial support system, if he had suffered severe brain damage and/or the chances of his recovering consciousness were regarded as minimal. The effect of removing the support systems may be that he will die; or he may live for some time in an unconscious state, breathing on his own. If the patient dies, the medical action of removing the support systems could be described as euthanasia, but it does not fit easily into either a direct/indirect or active/passive categorisation. (Type 3)

Fourth, there is the deliberate withholding of medical treatment from a patient when death is thought to be very near or her quality of life is considered very poor. For instance, a routine course of antibiotics is often withheld when an old woman in the last stages of dying from cancer contracts pneumonia. This is sometimes described as 'passive' or 'negative' euthanasia. (Type 4)

In addition, all these forms of treatment or non-treatment can be applied either to patients who have requested such action or to those who have not. In the case of a comatose patient, of course, the only way that the patient could make such a request is at an earlier stage in life, *i.e.*, viewing the situation hypothetically. But the possibility of practising euthanasia on those who have not requested it has also arisen in relation to very young children, the mentally handicapped and the severely senile. So there is another important distinction to note, that between 'voluntary' and 'involuntary' euthanasia.

Furthermore, whatever one's final verdict on the ethics of euthanasia, the motive behind euthanasia is presumed to be a positive one. There is the assumption that because the patient is in great pain or because his chances of restoration to anything like a reasonable quality of life are minimal, it is to his benefit to die. In short, he is better off dead. Euthanasia means, literally, 'dying well'. The demand for it springs from humanitarian concerns.

Nevertheless, as I said in my opening paragraph, confusion reigns. For not everyone involved in the debate is prepared to use the word euthanasia of all the types of medical action or non-action which I have described. In particular, those who see themselves as disapproving of euthanasia (*i.e.*, those for whom euthanasia has an overwhelmingly bad connotation) tend to reserve the word for the first type of action, 'direct' or 'active' euthanasia.

For instance, the Anglican Board for Social Responsibility report *On Dying Well* says that where doctors use drugs to control pain even at the risk of shortening life (my type 2), or where a patient *in extremis* is not subjected to troublesome treatments which cannot restore him to health (my type 3 or 4), euthanasia is not involved.[1] Again, with regard to type 4, 'It is entirely misleading to call decisions to cease curative treatment "negative euthanasia"; they are part of good medicine, and always have been.'[2] In a similar vein, Dr Patrick Dixon writes as follows in *The Truth About AIDS:*

> Making a carefully planned decision not to start a particular treatment, or to stop one that may be artificially prolonging life or directly causing distress, in

---

[1] *On Dying Well: An Anglican Contribution to the Debate on Euthanasia,* CIO, 1975, p.8.

[2] *Op, cit.,* p.40.

someone who is near death and for whom the
possibility of recovery is extremely remote, is not
euthanasia. It is an essential part of good
management.[3]

I must confess that I do not find the practice of *defining*
certain courses of action as 'good medicine' or 'good
management', over against euthanasia which is considered
to be a bad thing, very helpful. If certain practices are good
medicine, why should they not constitute types of
euthanasia which are justified as distinct from types of
euthanasia which are not? Yet the fact is, despite the
positive literal meaning of the word, that euthanasia does
have very negative connotations for a significant number of
people. I am therefore inclined to put the word euthanasia
on one side as much as possible, to describe the different
types of medical action/non-action in straightforward
factual terms and then to argue for their justification or
otherwise without having the 'is this or is this not
euthanasia?' question hung like an albatross round one's
neck.

I shall call these different types of action death-inducing
(Type 1), pain-reducing (Type 2), support-withdrawing
(Type 3) and treatment-withholding (Type 4).

The Traditional View
As the quotations from *On Dying Well* and Dixon's book
have already indicated, there is a widespread view that
whereas actions of types 2,3 and 4 may in certain
circumstances be justifiable, the deliberate inducing of
death is not. This view can be described as the
mainstream Western medical view on the ethics of
euthanasia. In recent years there have been an increasing
number of dissentients from it, particularly in the country of
Holland, but it still has strong backing from the pillars of

---

3 Dr Patrick Dixon, *The Truth about AIDS*, Kingsway, 1987, p.128.

the medical establishment in this country. The reluctance
to take action which deliberately induces death is based on
a conviction which lies deeply embedded in Western
culture, and has been nurtured to a very large extent by
the Christian tradition. The conviction is that the
intentional killing of innocent humans is always wrong.
('Innocent' does not mean sinless, of course, but blameless
of any offence for which one deserves to be put to death by
a fellow-human.) However, the mainstream Western
medical view has not held as a corollary that all possible
steps to keep a patient alive as long as possible should be
taken in all cases. It has recognised a place for 'allowing to
die', notably when the struggle to cure a fatal illness has
been lost and death within a short period of time seems
certain. There comes a point in the course of a fatal illness
when the doctor's duty to the patient is no longer to make
every conceivable effort to preserve his life, but rather to
concentrate on care and making his experience of dying as
comfortable and pain-free as he can. Letting die, which is
seen as morally acceptable and indeed 'good medicine', is
therefore distinguished sharply from killing, which is seen
as morally unacceptable and the antithesis of good
medicine.

This mainstream view was evoked by Sir Douglas
Black, President of the Royal College of Physicians when
speaking at the trial of Dr Leonard Arthur: 'I distinguish
between allowing to die and killing. It is a distinction that
is sometimes difficult to defend in logic, but I agree it is
good medical practice not to take positive steps to end
life.' [4]

The words 'difficult to defend in logic' are interesting.
Could it be that this widespread conviction that there is a

---

[4] As quoted in the Linacre Centre Working Party Report,
*Euthanasia and Clinical Practice: Trends, Principles and
Alternatives,* 1982, p.87.

decisive moral distinction between killing and allowing to die rests more on intuition than reason? Such is the argument of the philosopher James Rachels in *The End of Life : Euthanasia and Morality*.[5] He defines our intuitions, plausibly enough, as 'our pre-reflective beliefs about what is right or wrong in individual cases - one might say, inelegantly, that they are our gut feelings'.[6] But Rachels thinks that our intuitions may be wrong. He puts a much greater trust in rational arguments. If even our deeply cherished moral intuitions cannot stand up to the force of rational argument, then we should be prepared to abandon them. And the decisive moral distinction between killing and letting die is one which he finds impossible to defend logically. In this he has the agreement of a number of other notable moral philosophers (*e.g.*, John Ladd, Peter Singer [7] as well as the supporters of the Voluntary Euthanasia Society.)

Criticisms of the Traditional View

Rachels and Ladd have some powerful points on their side. First, they argue that in taking a decision not to pursue a particular course of action one can be as responsible for what follows as in taking a decision *to* do it. This becomes clear in a situation where evil motives are obviously at work. Rachels uses the example of two men, Smith and Jones, who both desire the death of their six-year-old cousin in order to gain a large inheritance. Smith drowns his cousin by actively and deliberately pushing the child under the bath water. Jones plans to do the same thing, but is spared the necessity by his cousin slipping, hitting his head, and falling under the water; Jones watches the incident and makes no attempt to save the child. Is Jones

---

5 See James Rachels, *The End of Life: Euthanasia and Morality*, OUP, 1986, ch.8.

6 *Op. cit.*,p.130.

7 See John Ladd (ed.), *Ethical Issues Relating to Life and Death*, OUP, 1979, which includes an essay by Peter Singer.

in any significant degree less responsible for his cousin's death than Smith? He could hardly excuse his conduct by saying that he let nature take its course. He had the opportunity to save his cousin's life, but because of his evil motives, chose to forego that opportunity.

In a similar way (though now assuming the absence of any evil motives) a doctor cannot ignore the fact that a decision to withdraw support or withhold treatment is a responsible action which is likely to bring forward the time of his patient's death. Assuming that the patient has an incurable injury or illness, one may fairly say that she died of brain failure or cancer or whatever, but the doctor can certainly affect the timing of death. By leaving her on a life-support machine or by giving her antibiotics when she catches pneumonia on top of her cancer, he could prolong her life. Through taking an action not to do something, or not to go on doing it, the doctor must accept some responsibility (whether that be culpable or praiseworthy) for events which follow.

Second, an absolute bar on killing innocent persons seems to break down in the face of the most extreme forms of suffering. *On Dying Well* recognises that there are extreme situations outside the medical field (and where there is no ready access to medical aid) in which mercy-killing is a plausible moral option. The Working Party which wrote it considered 'cases, such as are occasionally reported in the newspapers, of drivers who have been trapped in vehicles which have caught fire after accidents and who have begged the bystanders to kill them as painlessly as possible so that they will not burn to death as is otherwise inevitable. In war, similar cases occur of men trapped in blazing gun turrets, and of wounded who face death by torture if left on the battlefield'.[8] If death is inevitable, and if aid is unavailable, then it does seem a

---

8 *On Dying Well*, p.10.

right because merciful thing to do to put someone out of
their misery in such situations. A prohibition on the
intentional killing of human beings is an excellent general
rule, but in view of such situations, we should hesitate to
accord it absolute status. In my book *Dilemmas* I argue in
favour of a more universal, if also more flexible principle,
'Never directly harming an innocent person', because it
does allow for the possibility that killing someone might
(just occasionally) be to their benefit rather than (much
more typically) to their harm.[9] And if - an important if -
there are some fatal medical conditions so painful and so
clearly beyond the ability of medical staff to alleviate in
any significant way, then the possibility of justification for
death-inducing action in such circumstances should be
taken seriously.

Third, Rachels and others make a weighty point when
they argue that a readiness to let die rather than to kill is
likely to lead to an increase in the patient's suffering. If we
withhold treatment from a terminal cancer-patient in
horrible pain, 'it may take him *longer* to die, and so he will
suffer *more* than he would if we were to administer the
lethal injection.'[10] This appears unhumanitarian. If we have
stopped giving him treatment, this is presumably because
we think that death is the best thing that can happen to
him; but because of our scruples about actively killing him,
we perpetuate his misery by days or weeks. Again, this
looks like a telling point against the traditional ethic.

In the light of these considerations, the case for
voluntary euthanasia, even of the death-inducing type
about which there is no argument that it constitutes
euthanasia, is not to be discounted too readily. The

9 Richard Higginson, *Dilemmas: A Christian Approach to Moral
   Decision-Making*, Hodder & Stoughton, 1988, pp.187-191.

10 James Rachels, 'Euthanasia, Killing and Letting Die', in John
    Ladd, *op. cit.*, pp.151-2.

distinction between killing and letting die is not so morally decisive as has often been alleged in this country. In Holland, the medical practice of deliberately inducing death by the use of barbiturates and other drugs is now widespread. This is not to say that such practice is legal, but since 1981, non-prosecution of doctors for this type of euthanasia is normal so long as they follow guidelines laid down by the Rotterdam Criminal Court, *e.g.* there must be physical or mental suffering which the patient finds unbearable; the suffering and desire to die must not be merely temporary; the decision to die must be the voluntary decision of an informed patient, etc. A certain case law has thus been established and it is likely that before very long, the Dutch criminal law will come to coincide with it. Disturbing though this development sounds, could it be that the Dutch have courageously grasped the nettle in a way which we and other countries have failed to do? An article charting developments in Holland which appeared in *The Sunday Times*, 'The Last Appointment', lends credence to the case by describing some instances of horrible suffering in which the participants resorted to the deliberate induction of death. For instance, there is Gerrit, a 55-year-old policeman who develops cancer in his bladder. It spreads relentlessly. He is forced to live with a colostomy bag and the pain grows steadily worse. Finally, the doctors announce that they will have to amputate his penis. Then there is Dirk, a 62-year-old lorry driver, who suffers from cancer which affects his face and eventually makes a hole the size of a fist by his nose.[11] In each case, radiation and chemotherapy had clearly failed. Should we really begrudge Gerrit and Dirk the massive dose of drugs which put them out of their misery?

---

11 'The Last Appointment', *Sunday Times Magazine* 7/6/87, pp.13-22.

I certainly find myself in sympathy with Dr Leo Fretz, president of the Dutch Society for Voluntary Euthanasia, when he says that 'from a moral point of view I think that voluntary euthanasia is less radical than some cases of abortion.'[12] At least with voluntary euthanasia the focus of concern is upon the person who will suffer death, *i.e.*, the concern is to release him from his suffering. In many (surely most) cases of abortion, the focus of concern is not upon the person who will suffer death (the unborn child) but upon those who will be affected - apparently adversely - by the advent of the child. It is not usually the interests of the child that those who desire an abortion have at heart. Yet Britain's medical establishment goes along with abortion but staunchly resists euthanasia. Is there not a strange loss of moral perspective here?

A Christian Perspective

What does Christian theology have to say about this issue? As we have noted, the mainstream Western view which has renounced killing, but accepted the practice of allowing to die, has been strongly influenced by Christian tradition. It is not difficult to see why. In *Dilemmas* I characterise the Christian attitude to life and death as a readiness to accept both in a positive spirit.[13] St Paul memorably expresses this attitude in the words of Philippians 1:21, 'For me to live is Christ, and to die is gain'. On the one hand, Christians regard life as a gift from God, a state of being which we should hold sacred and seek to preserve. On the other hand, death too can be a gift from God, a merciful release to a life beyond suffering, and so it should not be viewed as an enemy to be kept at bay at all costs. A balanced view of this sort points to the appropriateness of a medical policy which seeks to save

---

12 As quoted in 'The Last Appointment', p.18.

13 See *Dilemmas*, p.195.

life whenever the prognosis gives cause for hope, but is ready to accept death when the prospects are dire.

For the Christian, the suffering and pain which may give rise to thoughts about euthanasia represents a challenge to her faith. They may at times lead the sufferer to doubt the goodness, even the existence of God; but they can also lead the sufferer to an increased dependence on God and a more vivid awareness of his presence which both reduces and transcends the suffering. Suffering may also be an experience in which one is either disappointed or comforted depending on the love and concern shown by fellow-humans. The suffering associated with dying is likely to be an especially profound experience, either for good or ill. Is one not cutting oneself off from what is potentially a very rich experience if one asks someone else to curtail one's life? In particular, it is surely better to end life on earth in a spirit of utter dependence on God, rather than by committing an act which is a radical assertion of one's autonomy.

A paragraph in *On Dying Well* is worth quoting in this context : 'The value of human life consists in a variety of virtues and graces as well as in pleasure. These together constitute man's full humanity. They grow in soil in which action and passion, doing and suffering, pleasure and pain are intermixed. What a man is consists not only of what he does, but also of how he endures. A fully human life is inescapably vulnerable, as every lover knows, and even suffering may by grace be woven into the texture of a larger humanity... Even dying need not be simply the ebbing away of life; it may be integrated into life, and so made instrumental to a fuller life in God.'[14]

---

[14] *On Dying Well*, p.21

I am sure that these arguments are persuasive for the vast majority of cases in the Western world today. The suffering which is associated with death is suffering which still carries with it creative possibilities. But some suffering may not be of this order. If one is suffering from an illness for which no satisfactory pain control has been discovered, or is faced by a prospect which appears cruelly humiliating (like the amputation of Gerrit's penis), or has experienced a disfiguration which repels even one's friends and relatives so that they can no longer bear to visit (like the hole in Dirk's face), is one not coming to the limits of the tolerable? To say 'I cannot bear this; please have mercy and kill me' is not necessarily a denial of one's dependence on God or a usurpation of his sovereignty. It could be a humble act, a confession of one's limits, or a wish to preserve in death a semblance of human dignity which we are after all accustomed to call God-given. Because of this possibility, I believe that it is wrong to take an absolute moral stance against euthanasia. Granted that the thrust of Christian theology is opposed to it, there *are* exceptional situations where a strong moral case can be made for taking life. The mainstream Western view warrants some qualification.

Qualifications to the Qualification
Nevertheless, in thinking about this issue, it is important to proceed with care. Thus far I have put the case for selective voluntary euthanasia in as positive a light as I feel able. But even the strongest points made by its advocates require some qualifications.

I have argued earlier that in taking a decision to withdraw support or withhold treatment, a doctor can play as responsible and significant a part in determining the time of a patient's death as a doctor who induces death directly through the administration of drugs. But the doctor does not most likely *seek* the death of the patient, nor will he usually *know* that the patient will die imminently with anything like the same certitude. When Dr Pieter Admiraal of the Delft General Hospital injects a patient with barbiturates, often throwing in a dose of curare for good measure, he anticipates the death of the patient within a couple of days with some confidence. Additional injections are likely to be applied if the patient shows signs of lingering on unduly. But when a comatose patient comes off a life support machine or an old woman with cancer is not given antibiotics for her pneumonia, it is much more unpredictable how long they will survive. Karen Quinlan, the comatose American girl about whom a contentious legal battle raged in the 1970's, surprised her physicians by living for several years in an unconscious state after her respirator had been turned off. In taking a decision to withdraw support or withhold treatment, a doctor *may* be trying to hasten the moment of death (and his action will often have that effect). But it could rather be that he is no longer seeking to prolong life. Similarly, a patient's request that certain treatments be withheld may have the same orientation. The nuance may seem to be a fine one, but both doctor and patient should know if they are actively seeking death by the yardstick of whether they feel disappointed when the patient continues to live!

Moreover, while I have acknowledged the possibility of euthanasia being justified in circumstances of extreme pain, it is doubtful whether this pain has to be a reality because of the developments in modern medicine. Drugs can dull the pain significantly for patients with most types of medical condition. The hospice movement has led the way in refining the art of using pain-killing drugs; it has to be said of many of the horror-stories produced by advocates of voluntary euthanasia that the scope exists within medical care to handle the situation better. Nevertheless, with unusual types of illness or where the pain is especially acute or chronic, medical science may still be able to do little - little, that is, except sedate a patient so heavily that he is rendered unconscious for long periods of time. The larger the dose given, of course, the greater is the possibility that doctors may end up bringing about the patient's death indirectly. Christian ethicists have long defended such treatment on the grounds of double effect, the principle which says that one is justified in permitting incidental evil effects from one's good actions if there is a proportionate reason for doing so. Reasonably enough, the crucial moral question is seen as what the doctor intends, whether it is to kill the pain or kill the patient.

This brings me to a third important qualification to my limited espousal of the euthanasia cause. I do think that we need to take what actions *feel* like to the medical personnel concerned seriously. It is tempting to deride the Sir Douglas Blacks of this world as muddle-headed and there are certainly logical grounds for arguing, as I have done, that the distinction between killing and letting die is not so clear-cut as has often been imagined. But taking active steps to finish a patient off certainly feels very different from refraining from a particular course of treatment to most doctors involved. There is a considerable psychological gulf between the different types of action which might all be described as euthanasia. In connection with this, if the sphere of medical care comes to include the deliberate inducing of death, this does involve a radical reshaping of the task of medicine. The doctors' task takes on a new dimension - killing - alongside those of caring, curing and alleviating suffering. It is understandable that most appear reluctant to make this jump. Again, public comprehension of the role of the medical profession would surely change, and in some cases, might well lead to apprehension, doctors being seen in a much more ambivalent light than they are at present.

It is of course true that with regard to one particular class of patients some members of the medical profession are already regularly involved in the practice of killing. I refer to unborn children and the practice of abortion. If doctors have made an exception to the 'no killing' rule in this area, why not, one may say, in another? However, while I regret the development of widespread abortion, I do not think that it alters the doctor's role to anything like the same extent that acceptance of euthanasia would. Abortion is practised on individuals who (though in my view, fully human and truly personal) are not themselves known by others, nor can they anticipate what is about to happen to them. The direct killing of individuals who are known and familiar members of society, by doctors who are members of one of the most respected professions, would make a much greater impact.

Reasonable Pain Threshold and Individual Autonomy

The Voluntary Euthanasia Bills which have been unsuccessfully presented to Parliament have differed in the way they have been phrased. In the 1936 Bill, euthanasia was to be restricted to patients suffering from a disease which was 'incurable, fatal and painful'. It was assumed that such action would be contemplated only in the terminal stage of such an illness. The 1969 Bill provided that a patient or prospective patient should be able to sign in advance a declaration requesting the administration of euthanasia if he was believed to be suffering from 'a serious physical illness or impairment reasonably thought in the patient's case to be incurable and expected to cause him severe distress or render him incapable of rational existence'. The difference in wording is notable in two respects. It was now considered sufficient that the illness was incurable; it need not necessarily be fatal; and the category of 'incapacity for rational existence' was added to that of 'expected to cause severe distress'. If the 1969 Bill had become law, a woman who develops a serious eye condition, leading to loss of her sight, could request euthanasia, even though blindness is not a terminal illness; and a man who goes senile could also (because he has previously requested it) be put to death, even though senility might for him be a pain-free existence. Clearly there is scope in euthanasia legislation for the gateway to a deliberately induced death to be opened very wide indeed.

Within the Voluntary Euthanasia Society at present, there appears to be either unclarity or a difference of opinion as to when euthanasia might legitimately be requested. In its literature, the Society claims that the primary aim throughout its history has been 'to bring about a situation where any responsible adult, suffering from a fatal and distressing illness for which no relief is known, can receive an immediate painless death if, *and only if,* that is his or her considered choice'. Here, the word 'fatal' is included. But the Voluntary Euthanasia Bill which they favour at present speaks of a condition diagnosed as 'irremediable', this being defined as a 'serious and distressing physical illness or impairment from which the patient is suffering without reasonable prospect of cure'. Moreover, in the VES Newsletter for January 1988, John Beloff, Chairman of the Voluntary Euthanasia Society for Scotland, wrote that there were three main contingencies as a result of which he would not want to go on living. These were (i) if he faced a complete loss of memory (ii) if he could no longer control his bladder and bowels and (iii) if he were no longer able to feed himself or perhaps even if he could no longer enjoy his food.[15] None of these have anything necessarily to do with a terminal illness.

What one finds in the VES literature are two contrasting emphases. The first emphasises the awfulness of the suffering still experienced by many patients. Implicitly it appeals to a pain threshold and suggests that it is unreasonable to expect human beings to endure life

---

[15] The Voluntary Euthanasia Society literature quoted here is obtainable from their headquarters, 13 Prince of Wales Terrace, London, W8 5PG

beyond this threshold. Although I think it is very difficult to identify exactly where this threshold lies (since a person's capacity to endure pain clearly varies quite markedly) I have some sympathy with this viewpoint. The second line of argument emphasises the autonomy of the individual patient. It is for the patient to decide when she has had enough; she has the right to choose, and that includes the right to die at a time of her choosing. Here, the emphasis is on individual rights and the question of the severity and finality of the illness from which a patient suffers recedes into the background. Indeed, if it was to be conceded that individuals have a right to die simply by virtue of their autonomy, then why need this right be linked to their suffering physical illness at all? Why should not an individual who was simply dissatisfied with life, or perhaps had a penchant for the theatrical, simply demand that his doctor accede to his wish to die with no further explanation required?

It is this second strand in the VES literature that I find quite unacceptable. There are two main reasons for this. First, it exalts individual freedom above a corporate commitment to the goodness of life. Most of us, most of the time, feel that life is worth living; whatever its pains and sorrows, its trials and tribulations, we feel that living has its compensations and its creative possibilities.

When somebody is so ill or so depressed that they no longer want to live, we believe that something is seriously awry and seek to change either their conditions or their attitude to life. We hope and trust that their wishing to die is a temporary episode which will pass. It is a mark of friendship and loyalty to stick by them during this episode rather than accede to what may after all be only a passing whim and collaborate in their suicide. It may of course be objected that the attitude I ascribe to 'we' is a rather paternalistic attitude, but I do not regard that as a damning indictment which ends the argument; better paternalism, I would say, than this abandonment of any idea of a shared moral consensus for a radical subjectivism. If society was to grant the availability of euthanasia purely on grounds of individual autonomy, the implication would be extremely serious: a significant reduction of social commitment to the basic desirability of living.

Second, the individual cannot pretend that what he does affects only himself and has no bearing on the wider society. Someone who commits suicide makes many people poorer and sadder by his loss. But someone who commits euthanasia actively involves other members of society, notably the medical profession, in bringing his death about. He asks others, on the grounds of their greater competence, to commit the decisive act. He may imagine that their complying to his request is a simple and straightforward matter - are the doctors not simply an extension of his will? - but that is not how it feels to them. They realise the momentous nature of what they are doing. Doctors in Holland who are prepared to take part in voluntary euthanasia procedures admit that it affects them deeply: 'You should never drive yourself to and from such an appointment - always make sure there is someone else, perhaps the other doctor, to drive you. It is too emotional, the chances are you will crash.'[16] Those who contemplate euthanasia in any except the extremities of pain and suffering need to remember what a burdensome responsibility they are asking someone else to carry.

If euthanasia is ever approved in this country, then, it should not be on the grounds of an individual's 'right to die'. It should be on the grounds of some shared social agreement that certain levels of human suffering are intolerable. But it is one thing to admit this as a theoretical possibility. The advocates of voluntary euthanasia are campaigning for a change in the law, and changes in the

---

[16] Dr Herbert Cohen quoted in 'The Last Appointment', p.16.

law have serious consequences. We need to think
carefully about what these might be.

Dangers in Legalising Euthanasia

Those who oppose the legalisation of voluntary euthanasia
have pointed out many undesirable consequences which
might follow a change in the law. Most of the points which
they make are weighty and substantial. I shall briefly
summarise the more important ones.

First, there is a problem in the elasticity of almost any
terms which might be used in the legislation. 'Serious
physical illness', 'incurable', 'incapable of rational
existence': none of these and similar concepts could be so
tightly defined as to eliminate argument about their
application. The pressure on doctors would be to interpret
them loosely, to push the boundaries out so that
eventually virtually any patient who wanted to die badly
enough could get his or her way. We have seen this
happen with the application of the Abortion Act. Risk to
the mental health of the woman has often been interpreted
along the lines of 'likely to cause stress and
inconvenience'; a substantial risk of a child being born
seriously handicapped can mean a less than 50% chance.
And what is 'seriously handicapped'? Some Spina Bifida
children only suffer from a very minor handicap, but the
practice of aborting fetuses diagnosed as being Spina
Bifida (and indeed Downs Syndrome) has become almost
routine. Similar laxity of interpretation could be anticipated
with any euthanasia legislation which might be passed.

Second, there is a problem about when is the
appropriate moment for requests for voluntary euthanasia
to be made. If doctors act on an advance declaration, there
is a danger of their abiding by what for the patient was an
entirely hypothetical exercise which no longer coincides
with their wishes, if they were in a fit state to
communicate them. If on the other hand they act on a

request made by the patient at the height of his suffering, they could be placing too much store by a passing mood. Cancer patients typically go through a series of stages: denial, anger, resentment, depression, and finally acceptance is how Hugh Trowell describes them.[17] It would be tragic if some patients were deprived of that final stage (in which, who knows, they might discover peace with God) if, because they had expressed a desire to die at an earlier stage of the saga, this wish had been all too quickly acted upon. Admittedly, the advocates of voluntary euthanasia try to provide some safeguards, *e.g.*, that a request to die should not be acted upon for 30 days and during that time the patient has a chance to revoke it. But the darkest phases of a serious illness can frequently last that long and still be succeeded by something better. Sufficient to say there are dangers here.

Third, there is a danger of pressures coming to bear upon patients to request euthanasia. These could take a variety of forms. In some cases, the patient's suffering may actually be felt more keenly by his friends and relatives than the patient himself. For instance, as onlookers we find it terrible to see someone whom we have known as a sane, healthy adult degenerate to a senile and incontinent condition; but precisely because of the loss of awareness caused by his brain deterioration, *he* may not mind being in that state as much as *we* mind him being in that state. Because of the horror and distaste his condition evokes in us, it is easy to convey a notion of 'your life isn't worth living' to the patient. Another pressure which may be felt by the patient is the feeling of being a terrible burden on her family, on the medical staff and on society as a whole; she may come to think it is selfish to be such a drain on their resources. Occasionally, of course, there could be sinister motives at work, like relatives' desire for financial

---

[17] See Hugh Trowell, *The Unfinished Debate on Euthanasia*, SCM Press, 1973, pp.102-108.

gain through the patient's death. In most cases, however, it can be anticipated that any pressure that others bring on a patient to request euthanasia would be unintended and indirect, but it could be no less real for that. And if the patient does then duly sign the form and is sent painlessly on his way, what then? Euthanasia might very well shorten the agony relatives experience in watching a loved one die, but it could also add to the feelings of guilt that are often felt in bereavement. They might now be saddled with remorse about having failed to show their loved one that they cared sufficiently - hence his opting to die.

A fourth danger is that certain groups in society might come to be identified as 'appropriate' for the practice of euthanasia. It is clear that in the treatment of severely handicapped children notions other than the purely medical (*i.e.*, what chance an operation has of improving the child's condition) often creep in. Where Downs children with a bowel obstruction have been refused this routine operation, it is clear that judgements about their quality of life or social utility have influenced doctors' or parents' thinking. With regard to euthanasia, the group that is increasingly likely to come under scrutiny is people with AIDS. Some AIDS victims, of course, have requested euthanasia. It is understandable why. AIDS has no known cure, it typically takes its victims through a variety of physical illnesses, some of which are very unpleasant, and people with AIDS often suffer from public attitudes because they are associated (in the West, at least) with homosexual practices. One is confronted not only with a terminal illness, but also - in many cases - with discrimination, suspicion and fear. Yet is is precisely because of these negative attitudes that I feel allowing people with AIDS to opt for euthanasia would be a retrograde step. It would encourage in the public a feeling that AIDS is a disease apart and that the lives of AIDS victims have no value. This in turn could make people with AIDS feel more wretched and lacking is self-respect. Our opinions of ourselves are very closely intertwined with the opinions of others; the value placed on our own life usually reflects the value attributed to it by others. Although the option of euthanasia for AIDS victims would be a welcome release to some, I believe that it would make matters worse for those AIDS victims who do want to go on living, to try to wrest some measure of satisfaction out of their remaining time on earth and to campaign for better treatment for themselves. They would have to contend with an additional obstacle, people refusing to listen because they think they should have done the decent thing and opted to die.

Of course, there is another major factor why euthanasia has been mooted in this context. That is the enormous cost of treating AIDS patients, whether that cost is incurred by the patient himself or by the state. This cost has to be taken seriously, but it raises huge questions about the proper funding and distribution of medical resources which lie outside the scope of this paper. Sufficient to say that I do not feel those working in the field of medical ethics should feel coerced in their judgements by constraints imposed by the present level of available resources. It is important to face the moral issue squarely (is it right to bring forward the moment of death for AIDS patients?) before moving on to the financial one. If it is very definitely not right, then the finances will need to be reassessed, taxes will have to be raised, *etc.*

A final danger about steps to legalise euthanasia is that they might lead to a loss in impetus of the movement towards better care for the dying. Thanks largely to the hospice movement, giant steps have been made in this area in the last two decades. The amount of pain has decreased and the quality of care increased for patients in many institutions and suffering from many types of illness. There remain institutions where improvements need to be made and illnesses which remain resistant to pain control.

If euthanasia were legalised, would the pressure to make continued progress lose momentum? I suspect it would. Another possible consequence might be that we become a society where nobody cared particularly about people committing suicide. This is linked to a point I made earlier, that we would have become a society reduced in our commitment to the basic desirability of living.

I am well aware that an advocate of euthanasia might say of all these possible scenarios: sure, these are possible consequences of a change in the law. But they are not necessary consequences. People might react differently from the way that I have suggested. The advocate of euthanasia is apt to object to 'slippery slope' or 'thin-end-of-the-wedge' arguments and say that the danger of a moral position's being abused should not deter one from taking up that position, if it is the right position. One should be prepared to observe and stick by appropriate distinctions. As far as our moral thinking in the abstract is concerned, I entirely agree with this objection. But thinking in a purely abstract way is exactly what one cannot afford to do when one comes to contemplate changing the law. In drawing new legal boundaries, nothing is more important than attention to possible abuses since one has to take seriously the response of a whole society to a particular law. The dangers to which I have drawn attention are not just possible ones, in my view, but very plausible ones. Philosophers, who live in a world of clear-cut distinctions, are not necessarily helpful law-makers for a society of people who make them less easily. I believe that David Lamb, a philosopher who does have his feet on the ground, is essentially correct:

> The significance of the (slippery) slope argument is in the way it reveals the inherent, but frequently overlooked, problems entailed in proposals to redraft the rules in order to accommodate what are currently regarded as ethically justifiable breaches of it...the

citing of exceptional cases where euthanasia might be morally defensible is no argument for a change in the law or for a re-drafting of our attitudes towards life. In such cases the law is best maintained, but with leniency and understanding.[18]

Concluding Thoughts

It is time to return to where I began, to the four types of action which might possibly be classed as euthanasia: death-inducing, pain-reducing, support-withdrawing and treatment-withholding. The traditional, Western and largely Christian view has classified the first type of action as euthanasia, and reprehensible; it has regarded the other three as acceptable in certain situations.

I wish to make some small but significant modifications to that view. The crucial criterion for deciding whether something constitutes euthanasia lies not in whether it is active or passive, not whether it is doing something or not doing it, but *whether the death of the patient is deliberately sought,* through whatever means. I agree with the substance of the admittedly clumsy definition found in the Linacre Centre's report *Euthanasia and Clinical Practice:* 'there is euthanasia when the death of a human being is brought about on purpose as part of the medical care being given him'.[19] According to this definition, type 1 definitely is euthanasia; types 3 and 4 might be, though more probably the decision will be one to cease futile treatment or cease trying to prolong life rather than deliberately seeking death; and type 2 is not, though where the dose given is sufficiently heavy one can conceive of motives becoming mixed or at least ambiguous.

---

18 David Lamb, *Down the Slippery Slope: Argung in Applied Ethics,* Croom Helm, 1988, p.121.

19 *Euthanasia and Clinical Practice,* p.2

Decisions to withdraw support or withhold treatment are justified where a patient can confidently be assessed as being in the final stages of dying. If the patient is suffering from acute as opposed to terminal illness, then these actions would be wrong. Gastric tubes, intravenous injections, antibiotics, respirators and cardiac resuscitation are all supportive measures for use in acute illnesses to help a patient through a critical period towards recovery of health. But where a patient is terminally ill and there is no prospect of even a partial recovery of health, doctors need not feel bound to resort to them. In Paul Ramsey's memorable phrase, there comes a stage when their responsibility is only caring for the dying.[20]

In certain extreme cases, it *might* be possible to find moral justification for a doctor to seek the death of a patient with the patient's support, by resorting to any of these types of action. I cannot rule out the possibility of some experiences of suffering so vile that *mercy*-killing would be a reality. But with the improving state of Western medicine, I feel these instances are very few, and I believe that the dangers which would attend a move to legalise euthanasia are so great that this step should not be taken.

I confess that this is a somewhat untidy conclusion. I wish to modify the absolute moral stance against euthanasia, I am blurring a clear-cut distinction between killing and allowing to die, yet I am standing firm in resisting change to the law. But then life often is untidy, never more so, perhaps, than when it concerns death.

---

[20] See Paul Ramsay, *The Patient as Person: Explorations in Medical Ethics,* Yale University Press, 1970, ch.3.

7

Life, Death and the Handicapped Newborn

C. Everett Koop

This paper was first published in Ethics and Medicine 3.2, 1987.

The death of handicapped newborn infants whether by withholding beneficial treatment, hydration, or nutrition, or by some direct act is extraordinarily important to those of us who are interested in the sanctity of human life because this practice could never have come about had it not been for abortion. I shall refer to this for brevity as infanticide although I realise that on this side of the Atlantic infanticide does not have exactly the same definition that we use.

By infanticide I will mean the deliberate killing, - because that is what it is, - of a newborn whether by an act of omission or a deliberate procedure that deprives the child of life.

When the Supreme Court of the United States in 1973 made abortion on demand the law of the land, it chilled some of us to read that the justice who wrote the majority opinion said that he considered the Hippocratic oath which forbids abortion to be irrelevant. He further stated that he spurned whatever morality might be gleaned from the Judaeo-Christian heritage of our country but instead turned to the pagan religions of Rome, Greece and Persia. Although those countries practised abortion, it was infanticide and euthanasia which were more important inhumanities in their culture.

It is important to remember that infanticide is euthanasia in a specific age group. Because infanticide gained such a foothold in our country in the 1960s and 1970s, I am afraid it will come back to haunt us some day when the forces of euthanasia have their way. I can almost hear their reasoning now: 'Why are you concerned about euthanasia? You've been practising it on newborns now for several decades.'

A third important thing about infanticide is that it is being practised by a segment of our population from which we should expect more and being ignored by others who should have more integrity. It is being practised by that segment of the medical profession which, in days gone by, we could always count upon to stand in the role of advocate for children.

Finally, infanticide is being ignored by the law. Infanticide is homicide. The law makes believe it does not happen.

It was really infanticide and all of its implications that brought me into the Pro Life Movement. For more than 34 years I devoted the major part of my professional life to the management of children who were born with congenital defects, many of them incompatible with life, but usually amenable to surgical correction.

Because I was the sixth person in our country to devote his surgical skills to children alone, then because I eventually became the Surgeon-in-chief of the oldest children's hospital in America, I probably did more newborn surgery than anyone in the country until the time that I was called by President Reagan to assume my present post.

Therefore, I know what can be accomplished in the way of rehabilitation of the child. I know what can be done with his family. I know these youngsters become loved and loving, that they are creative, and that their entrance into a family is frequently looked upon in subsequent years as an extraordinarily positive experience.

You might be interested in an anecdote from the early 1970s. My colleagues and I had spent an entire Saturday operating on three newborns with congenital defects lethal without surgical correction. We had successfully corrected the defects and at the end of the day sat down and with a great feeling of satisfaction said that we had given about 70 years of life to each of three children but *in toto* they weighed about ten pounds, all three of them together.

Then one of us said, Do you realise that while we have spent the day doing this, right next door they have killed babies of the same size who were perfect, just because their mothers didn't want them?

I went home that night, tired as I was, and began to write a book, *The Right to Live, the Right to Die*, which I finished by Monday morning.

The argument is frequently made by people who have never had the privilege of working with handicapped children who are being rehabilitated into our society after correction of a congenital defect, that such infants should be allowed to die or even encouraged to die because their lives could obviously be nothing but unhappy and miserable.

Yet, it has been my constant experience that disability and unhappiness do not go hand in hand. Some of the most unhappy children I have known have been completely normal. On the other hand there is a remarkable joy and happiness in the lives of most handicapped children. Some have borne burdens cheerfully which I would have found difficult to face, indeed.

With the affluence of our society, we are really seeing only the beginning of what can be done for handicapped youngsters, both technically and medically, as well as in their pursuit of leisure activity. Who knows what happiness is for another person? What about rewards and satisfaction in life for those who work with and succeed in their rehabilitation of handicapped children? Stronger character, compassion, deeper understanding of another's burdens, creativity and deeper family bonds - I'm convinced that all of these attributes result from this so-called social burden of raising a child that is less than perfect.

There is also no doubt in my mind that the value placed upon the patient by his associates, as one who is respected, honoured and loved is a source of inspiration to all who see it.

The first film in our country on the subject of infanticide was produced by Johns Hopkins Hospital and Medical School in Baltimore and was entitled, 'Who shall survive?'

This was not a motion picture scenario. It was filmed in real life and real time. It depicted a mother who had just given birth to a child who had a simple intestinal obstruction that could have been corrected with a 45 minute procedure and a 99 per cent success rate. Unfortunately, the youngster also had Down's Syndrome and the mother did not want a retarded child. After discussion by the medical staff, the nursing staff, the social service workers, a psychiatrist and a chaplain, it was decided by all of these that the child should die. A sign was hung on the foot of the bed which said 'Nothing by mouth', and the crib was put in a corner. Fifteen days later a parched, emaciated, little infant died, too weak to cry.

The Foundation which provided the money for that film had as its intent to show the horror of infanticide. Instead, that film has been used in medical schools in the United States to teach young medical students and physicians how to handle the problems of a child who is not deemed worthy of life.

The first medical article along these lines appeared in the prestigious *New England Journal of Medicine* under the title, 'Dilemmas of the Newborn Intensive Care Nursery,' and was authored by Professor Raymond Duff and Professor A. J. M. Campbell, both of Yale University. They acknowledged that over a two-year period 14 per cent of the deaths in that unit were deaths that they permitted to happen because it was their considered judgment after discussion with the family that these children had lives not worth living.

Here are several statements they make in support of their position: 'Survivors of these neonatal intensive care units may be healthy and their parents grateful, but in some instances they continue to suffer from such conditions as chronic pulmonary disease, short bowel syndrome, or various manifestations of brain damage.'

Duff and Campbell also said: 'Often too, parents' and siblings' rights to relief from seemingly crushing burdens were an important consideration in our decision.'

It's odd that Duff and Campbell talk about these parents who have entered into a conspiracy to kill their child, having deeper meaning in their lives after this experience. Could it not be that if they were seeking deeper meaning in their lives they might have better found it in taking care of the child that had been given to them?

Although Duff originally just withheld feeding from these patients, toward the end of that awful era he was giving parents morphine to administer to their own children after he had discharged them to home care.

Another voice at the same time came from Arthur Dyck of Boston, Professor of Population Ethics at Harvard School of Public Health, who said: 'The moral question for us is not whether the suffering and dying are persons, but whether we are the kind of persons who will care for them without doubting their worth.'

Professor Dyck believes in the equality of life rather than the quality of life ethic. I agree with him. So did Hippocrates.

I would not have you believe that everyone in our country feels that way. Even two physicians who worked right in the same unit with Duff and Campbell wrote a letter to the journal that published their paper and said the following: 'As consultants to the Newborn Special Care Unit, we wish to disassociate ourselves from the opinions expressed by the authors. The growing tendency to seek early death as a management option that the authors referred to has been repeatedly called to the attention of those involved and has caused us deep concern. It is troubling to us to hear young paediatric interns ask first,

'Should we treat?' rather than 'How do we treat?'.We are fearful that this feeling of nihilism may not remain restricted to the Newborn Special Care Unit. To suggest that the financial and psychological stress imposed upon a family with the birth of a handicapped child constitutes sufficient justification for such a therapy of nihilism is untenable and allows us to escape what perhaps after all are the real issues - the obligation of an affluent society to provide financial support and opportunity for a gainful life to its less fortunate citizens.'

I don't know what proportion of health professionals in the United States feel as I do about the withholding of beneficial treatment from handicapped newborns, but I do know that the vocal ones, or at least those that are reported in the Press, are not on my side.

One of the best words of wisdom on this subject was given by Professor John A. Robertson, then of the University of Wisconsin Law School, who said this: 'One must decide for whose benefit is the decision to withhold treatment from a child with severe birth defects. Is no life better than one of low quality? The person to ask is an individual who has a disabling birth defect.'

I did just that with some of my patients. The patients at the time ranged in age from eleven to thirty years. One patient had been born with a number of major congenital defects down the midline of his body requiring thirty-seven operative procedures for correction. Another was born without an oesophagus, requiring transplantation of the colon to replace that absent organ. Still another was born with a tumour of the tongue necessitating almost total amputation of that structure in a series of operations. The final youngster with congenital defects was born with major defects of the oesophagus, no rectum, and no innervation of the bladder.

The other four children all had tumours. One was a benign tumour of the bones of the face, which had required a number of operations for correction and we still had not achieved perfection. The other three had cancers of the adrenal gland, of the parotid gland, and of the uterus. There can be no doubt about how such young people feel about the joy of living, despite the time-consuming and usually painful medical and surgical procedures they have endured to correct birth defects or those discovered in early childhood. Here is a sampling of their comments:

Because the start of life was a little abnormal, it does not mean you are going to finish that way. I am a normal functioning human being, capable of doing anything anybody else can.

At times it got very hard, but life is certainly worth living. I married a wonderful guy and I am just so happy.

At the beginning it was a little difficult going back to school after surgery but then things started looking up with a little perseverance and support. I am an anaesthetist and I am happily married. Things are going great for me.

I really think that all my operations and all the things I had wrong with me were worth it, because I really enjoy life and I don't let the things that are wrong with me bother me.

If anything, I think I have had an added quality to my life - an appreciation of life. I look forward to every single morning.

Most of the problems are what my parents went through with the surgery. I have now been teaching high school for eight years and it is a great joy.

They spend millions of dollars to send men to the moon. I think they can spend any amount necessary to save someone's life. The human life is so important because it is a gift - not something you can give so you really don't have the right to take it either.

I really don't consider myself handicapped. Life is just worth living. What else can I say?

Two Nobel laureates have voiced opinions concerning this subject of infanticide although they did not include that word in their statements. James Watson of DNA Double Helix fame said:

If a child were not declared alive until three days after birth, then all parents could be allowed the choice only a few are given under the present system. The doctor could allow the child to die if the parents so choose and save a lot of misery and suffering. I believe this view is the only rational, compassionate attitude to have.

That was in May 1973. In January 1978 Francis Crick, was quoted in the *Pacific News Service* as saying:

No newborn infant should be declared human until it has passed certain tests regarding its genetic endowment and that if it fails these tests, it forfeits the right to live.

Before, during and after the activities just described in America, the same thing was going on here.

In Sheffield Mr Robert Zachary and Dr John Lorber were a team making great strides in the treatment of spina bifida. Suddenly Lorber changed his mind and became the chief exponent of infanticide in Great Britain. He was a very convincing spokesman. He travelled throughout the

Dr Lorber began his presentation with a dissertation on the beneficial advances in recent medical history that are allowing many people to live in an integrated society who formerly would have died or suffered severely. He then distinguishes this from the indiscriminate use of medicine which keeps alive many people who have by his definition no hope of becoming independent functioning members of society.

When I read British statistics that 100 per cent of the patients not treated by surgery in the first few days of life died, I know that they did not die from natural causes. They were either sedated so they could not drink or eat or they actually were given increasing doses of morphine to prevent the pain which almost all neurologists agree does not exist in these youngsters.

Listen to Dr Lorber's explanation:

This is where medical science has led us in the seventies. I show you these children not to horrify you or to make you faint but to make you understand why it is that I prefer the policy of selected treatment rather than creating this immense misery for such an immense number of individuals. We had to restore the balance.

Those who are severely affected from birth get worse and worse. Humanity demands that such badly affected infants should not be put through such constant severe punishment. Criteria had to be found, preferably on the first day of life, which could reliably separate those infants who may die early but even more importantly those who would live but would suffer from severe multisystem handicaps and would be unable to live an independent and dignified existence in spite of the best possible treatment. Such a selection is easily possible.

Hear how Dr Lorber sets the death sentence: 'It is essential that those who are not treated should not live long. It is imperative, therefore, that non-treatment should really be non-treatment, not just no operation. Nothing should be done to prolong life.'

There was another side. One of your eminent surgeons, Robert B. Zachary, in the Forshall Lecture given before the British Association of Paediatric Surgeons in 1976 said this:

> I believe that our patients, no matter how young or small they are, should receive the same consideration and expert help that would be considered normal in an adult. Just because he is small, just because he cannot speak for himself, this is no excuse to regard him as expendable, any more than we would do so on account of race or creed or colour or poverty. Nor do I think we ought to be swayed by an argument that the parents have less to lose because he is small and newborn, and has not yet established a close relationship with them, or indeed because the infant himself does not know what he is losing, by missing out on life.

Professor Rickham of Liverpool addressed the issue in an address on the 100th anniversary of the Sheffield Children's Hospital entitled, 'The Swing of the Pendulum'. .He said:

> How many normal newborn infants will live happily every after, especially in our present time? It may be argued that by not selecting, we artificially increase the number of people with an unhappy future, but can we be sure of this in any given case? After all, doctors deal with single, individual patients and not with statistical possibilities. It has also been pointed out that even a child with a grave physical and mental handicap can experience emotions such as happiness, fright,

gratitude and love and that it may be therefore, in fact, a rewarding task to look after him. It has been further argued that, strictly speaking, selection implies a limitation of resources, because with an optimum of resources and care a great deal can be done for these children and their families. In underdeveloped countries these resources do not exist, but in developed countries, where such enormous sums are spent by governments on purposes which are of a very doubtful benefit to humanity at large, the distribution of resources is a debatable subject. Finally, it can be argued that if selection is practised, it may not be necessarily the fittest on whom the greatest effort should be expended.'

On one occasion when Dr Lorber presented his material at a neurosurgical meeting in 1977, Dr John Freeman of Johns Hopkins spoke in response to Dr Lorber. Among his comments were these:

I don't know where he gets those slides of all those deformed human beings and indeed if the outcome were anything like what he presents, I would be standing beside him rather than opposite him. Selection takes many forms and I agree with selection, but I select a very small number, not 75 per cent. Selection takes many forms. But watch the terms. We are talking about selection for death, not university or college, a perversion, I think, of the term. We both believe strongly in discussing the prognosis with the parents. Yet, Dr Lorber's parents make diametrically opposite decisions to mine. Dr Lorber treats 25 per cent of the children brought to him: I treat 95 per cent. When a severely affected child with spina bifida is born, the question asked is, 'Should we do everything possible to maintain that child's life and make it the best life possible or is it best for that child to die? And that is the problem stripped of all the rhetoric.'

Withholding Treatment from Handicapped Newborns

In 1984, in the third year of his first term, President Ronald
Reagan did something unusual for a President - he wrote a
book, entitled *Abortion and the Conscience of the Nation*.
There were two additional chapters to that book entitled
'Afterwords.' One was by Malcolm Muggeridge. The other
I wrote some years earlier in 1977 entitled The Slide to
Auschwitz. My essay had to do with the then growing
practice of not feeding handicapped newborns because in
the eye of some beholders they did not have lives worthy
to be lived. It is not surprising then that the President was
incensed over the death of a child known only as 'Baby
Doe'.

Baby Doe was born at 8:19 a.m. on the 9th April 1982
which was Good Friday. He was cyanotic, that is his blood
was not properly oxygenated: he had an oesophagal
atresia, that is an obstruction in the oesophagus
incompatible with life but amenable to surgical correction:
and he had Down's Syndrome, a form of mental
retardation.

His obstetrician said he would be severely retarded,
something no one could possibly have known at that stage
of the child's development. He referred to the newborn as a
blob and he said that the mortality for the surgical
procedure to correct the oesophagus was fifty per cent. To
indicate how wrong that prediction was, I have repaired
475 such defects and in the last eight years of my practice
I never lost a full term baby and my survival for
prematures was 88 per cent.

There was also a paediatrician and a family practitioner
both of whom thought the child should be referred to the
nearest University Children's Hospital for surgical relief of
the obstruction. But the obstetrician advised the family to

refuse consent for surgery and told the family that the youngster would die in a few days from pneumonia.

At 9.30 a.m. on the same day the family took time out to think it over and at 10.00 a.m. decided: 'We do not want the baby treated.' The paediatrician asked if they realised what they were doing to which they replied 'Yes'. The obstetrician commented that the family had made a wise and courageous decision.

On April 10th, the following day, the obstetrician ordered the baby to be fed but told the nurses that this would result in choking and death. He forbade the use of IVs and ordered the child kept comfortable with sedation. The hospital administrator, fearing litigation, asked the family to take the baby home. They refused. The hospital attorney asked for a judicial hearing and the superior court judge said in view of the fact that there were two medical opinions, the parents could decide to take either one and inasmuch as they had already made that decision he would permit the child to die.

On Sunday 11th April the intensive care unit nurses revolted. The baby was transferred to a private room with private nurses and was given phenobarbital and morphine.

On Monday April 12th three attorneys sought to declare the child 'neglected' under the Child Abuse Statutes of the State of Indiana. The baby was now weak, parched, and spitting blood. At 11.00 p.m. on that date one of the lawyers sought a court order for intravenous feedings which was refused.

On Tuesday 13th several childless couples petitioned the court for adoption of the child which was denied. The interesting reason given was that it would look as if the family were abandoning the child rather than wanting it to die instead of living with its defects. Meanwhile the lawyers appealed to the Indiana Supreme Court, which without explanation refused to hear the case. On April 15th one of the lawyers was en route to Washington to file an appeal with the United States Supreme Court.

The hospital staff was in an uproar. The chief of staff ordered the paediatrician to start an IV and the altercation he would have had with the obstetrician who barred him from entering the patient's room was prevented by the death of Baby Doe at 10.01 p.m.

In spite of the tremendous things that have happened in the past half decade with organ transplantation, AIDS, new methods of health care financing and so on, there has been no area of public health policy that has stimulated such widespread discussion, such conflict - including law suits against the Government - and such profound change as this area labelled 'Baby Doe'.

The federal response to what happened to Baby Doe took two forms: first the Federal Government relied upon civil rights legislation first enacted in 1973 which prevented discrimination in the denial of medical treatment and nourishment to handicapped infants with life-threatening conditions. After the Government was successfully sued and regulations written to control the care of handicapped newborns were invalidated, Congress stepped in and enacted amendments to child abuse legislation that protected Baby Does under State Child Abuse Statutes.

There were non-binding interpretive guidelines accompanying the regulations which clarified the standard of 'medically beneficial treatment'. Treatments which 'are futile' or 'will do no more than temporarily prolong the act of dying of a terminally ill infant' were not required. Moreover, it was legitimate to withhold treatment if it was 'too unlikely of success given complications' or because it created 'risks' of potential harm to the infant.

If there were more than one reasonable course of treatment which would be medically beneficial, then medical judgement in selecting among treatments would be respected. In spite of the apparent deference to reasonable medical judgement there was underlined in the regulations a presumption in favour of treatment.

These guidelines were incorporated into the suggestion that hospitals with newborn intensive care nurseries set up patient care review committees and the response among medical institutions in the States was gratifying. In about a year and a half more than three-quarters of the hospitals with such units had patient care review committees, and most of the other hospitals either had combined one with another to have one committee for several hospitals or were in the process of forming a committee.

Having monitored the care of handicapped newborns probably as closely as anybody in the United States for the past twenty years, I would say in retrospect that probably the practice of withholding treatment and nutrition from handicapped newborns peaked out *before* Baby Doe was born and the practice had started to decline. With the adverse publicity about Baby Doe, especially in reference to the decision made by the physicians in charge, and with the subsequent regulations under Civil Rights authority, paediatricians began to rethink their position. What formerly was considered to be a broad grey area of dilemma in reference to decision-making was sharpened to a very narrow zone with black and white on either side.

Pro-Life organisations, the advocacy groups representing the handicapped, and the prestigious American Academy of Paediatrics joined together with me and Madeline Will, the Assistant Secretary for Education, and the compassionate care of handicapped newborns took a definite up-swing.

This improvement in care continued in spite of the regulations in reference to Civil Rights authority being found invalid by the United States Supreme Court and continued during the time of Congressional debate over protecting handicapped newborns under child abuse legislation. The situation was such that in late 1985 I said publicly that I thought handicapped newborns were better protected and better cared for than they had been in the previous decade and a half.

Now in spite of all the debates, public and private, despite the litigation which sharpened decision-making, both medically and legally, there isn't very much left in the way of statutory authority that can be enforced.

The child abuse amendments protecting handicapped newborns certainly represent a strong statement of national policy. This is particularly significant because the legislation was drawn up by a coalition of senators of Conservative and Liberal persuasion as well as Republican and Democratic affiliation. The House version of the same legislation was equally well represented.

The difficulty is that with fifty States with diverse child abuse regulatory procedures, the standard is probably not legally effective. Congress did stop short of demanding that the States conform with each other in statute and in regulatory action, as well as enforcement procedures.

You could say it in another way and that is that the legislation has imposed a standard of actions on hospitals and State child protective service agencies which is essentially unenforceable against individuals.

There are two options open. One is that the law can develop on its own at the State level and perhaps a standard which is uniform will be adopted, but that really requires cancellation of the federal standard. The other alternative is for Congress to strengthen its previous resolve and enact new legislation demanding a federal standard. Meanwhile, in the foreseeable future but not for too long, handicapped children are protected by personal reassessment of ethical positions by physicians, by general consensus that where we were in the years before Baby Doe was wrong, and of course in our country, unlike your own, there is the constant fear of litigation. The greatest protection that handicapped newborns have in the States today is the concern on the part of physicians and surgeons who care for newborns that someone is watching.

When the Baby Doe case first hit the newspapers, a number of people said the Government 'had no right' to interfere in a manner that was the responsibility only of the parents and of the attending physicians. Yet everyone knows that there are truancy laws and child abuse laws and immunisation laws and so on where the State's right to interfere is never seriously challenged. Those laws seem to be mainly accepted because for the most part they concern children who are no longer infants.

If the Baby Does of this world were thirty-five years old, they would have a national advocacy organisation and a strong Congressional lobby. Unfortunately they are too small, too weak, and too poor.

There is no constitutional definition of how old someone has to be in order to receive the protection of the State. There is no minimum age requirement for native born citizenship. For example, an American born child does not have to remain in the United States for a week . . . or two weeks . . . or even for an hour in order to qualify - thirty five years later - to run for President. The child merely has to be born an American. I don't find that difficult to understand. I never did. And following that same logic, I believe that a newborn infant whose life is put at risk by a parent, a guardian, a physician, or by whomever - I believe that child is a citizen and deserves to be accorded the full protection of the State.

Back in 1977, a journal, *Pediatrics*, published a survey made of two groups: one, the 400-member surgery section of the American Academy of Pediatrics; the other, a group of 300 persons who chaired departments or divisions of Paediatrics, Neonatology, and Genetics. They were asked a series of questions and it read almost like a friend of the court brief on Baby Doe, but of course this was five years earlier.

For example, they were asked, 'Would you acquiesce in the parents' decision to refuse consent for surgery in a newborn with intestinal obstruction if the infant also had Down's Syndrome alone?' Among the surgeons, 77 per cent would have acquiesced, 19 per cent would not. But the paediatric groups split on the question. Half said they would and half said they wouldn't. What if the parents decided that they did not want any corrective surgery done? Sixty-three per cent of the surgeons said they would then stop all supportive treatment; 31 per cent said they would continue to at least give oral feedings. However, only 43 per cent of the paediatric group would stop all supporting treatment . . . but they were generally unsure about what they would do instead. Only 18 per cent would give oral feedings.

But by far the largest number of responses to this and similar questions fell in the 'No answer' column.

I just don't believe that we can accept 'No answer' as an answer. Not from paediatricians - not from surgeons - not from the Government - and not from the public. If confronted by a newborn infant with one or more disabling conditions, each one of us must be prepared to respond - not take off and walk away. And that is the ethical issue we have got to deal with.

Baby Doe asks us to confess how we really feel about our fellow human beings. Baby Doe prods us into revealing whether we *are* - or *are not* - the friends of the helpless, the weak, the hurt, the injured, and the troubled.

The lives of health professionals as well as the lives of the parents and the disabled are remarkably shaped by the care we give the handicapped. I think that in my forty years of hands on experience has convinced me that all aspects of medical ethics are dwarfed by the question: 'How are we to care for those who cannot - in one way or in every way - care for themselves?'

When we have settled that question, then we can turn to the others such as finances, resources, committees and so on. No one said it would be easy. I am not even saying it can be objective. What I am saying is that the quality of life we talk so much about is nowhere as important as in the reflection these decisions make on the quality of our own lives.

8

Medical Aspects of Euthanasia

Duncan Vere

There has been so much confusion about the actual situations which obtain in medicinal therapy, and these confusions have been the ground of so many insecure proposals, that it seems right to start with some clarification.

The elements to be considered in any decision in medicinal therapy are these:

1. A treatment may be begun, or withdrawn.

2. Each choice in 1. could be made either to help, or to harm, a patient's prospects of survival.

3. A patient may be in a growth, slowly decrescent or steeply decrescent stage of natural life. Death is a natural part of life; it must not be prevented when it is the natural end of living.

4. A patient's illness may or may not already jeopardise his or her chance of survival - either naturally, or in relation to the probable outcome of therapy.

5. Treatment has several different outcomes; one concerns progression of the disease process, another concerns the likely adverse effects of therapy and a third concerns the quality of life during or after treatment.

6. Decisions about whether or not to treat, and with what measures, have always been jointly those of patient and doctor; but the balance of choice has shifted sharply in recent times. Doctors used to have the major, or even total role in such decisions. Their ethical grounds were (and are) largely consequentialist (*i.e.*, concerned with the probable outcomes for the patient). There is now a strong movement towards patient choice (subject autonomy) as the ethical ground for the decision. However, in almost all routine discussions of the subject the grounds of both patient and doctor are discussed purely as consequentialist or autonomous (*i.e.*, choice based on outcomes of whatever kind), and not on any deontological grounds of moral principle.

7. In terms of outcomes, major uncertainties exist. These are biostatistical, *i.e.*, outcomes of treatment follow a pattern indistinguishable from the apparently random responses of any biological system. Contrary to popular belief, no treatment is free from risk. Sometimes damage due to treatments arises not from faults in the remedy, but from unforeseeable disorders within the patient. But these uncertainties underlie a set of well-known pitfalls in the logic of treatment choice which might be called 'the doctors' dilemmas'. These are:

i) Once a patient is committed in therapy, there is no way of knowing what would have happened had therapy been withheld.

ii) Once treatment is chosen, there is no way to know what could have happened had another treatment been used.

iii) Once treated, a patient's improvement (or worsening) can be due either to natural processes or to therapy; it is often impossible to know to which cause the outcome may be attributed, without stopping treatment. If the benefit is natural, it is right to stop treatment; if the benefit is due to treatment, it is unethical to stop it. The ways in which treatment outcomes can be judged logically are discussed fully in a classical paper by Bradford Hill (1965). One disconcerting effect of these uncertainties is that whereas treatment choice often seems obvious *prospectively*, in retrospect it is easy to see that for that patient at that time the choice made was wrong, even disastrous or inept. Things can look very different, depending upon whether one's view is along or against time's arrow.

8.   It might seem, in view of such uncertainties, that doctors must make many mistakes. This is so, but it is fortunate that most medicinal therapy is *iterative, i.e.,* it proceeds step by step and, if the patient's responses are observed carefully, treatment plans can be revised in the light of outcomes; mistakes are corrigible. However, some outcomes are irreversible and incorrigible; it is obvious that a mistaken amputation cannot be corrected! Shortening life is always an incorrigible outcome of treatment.

9.   The social environment of treatment is one of the factors which must in part determine treatment choice. In all societies, the best treatments are available to only some people, at some times, because they cost so much. And societies vary enormously in the average levels of treatment they can afford. Equally, social conditions

determine whether therapies are practicable. Motor wheelchairs are useful only where there are roads; artificial kidneys are impossible to use under the conditions of a battlefield or major disaster. Treatments against infectious diseases work only when nutrition is good, and so on. This raises the whole field of preventive medicine (prophylaxis); by varying social conditions it is possible to avoid or avert the worst aspects of illness, in whole or in part.

10. The benefits and adversities of treatments do not depend only upon those treatments; they depend very much upon patients' expectations from therapy, or indeed from their illnesses for which therapy is given. These expectations are called their 'health belief models'. For example, it is well known that the amount of analgesia experienced by patients in pain depends very much upon their level of fear, and their expectations of relief from the drugs given to them. It is possible to lead patients to many kinds of expectations from their treatment. Doctors differ considerably in their reasons for starting treatment. Some place most weight upon the usual therapy for a disease state, and give it. Others weigh up the patients' personality, their needs and the severity of their problems, and prescribe only after considering these. Similarly, some patients always expect treatment as a routine, whereas others are more cautious in their acceptance of treatment. The most important point is that room must be left for a doctor's judgement; no doctor can be obliged to give treatment which he or she does not feel to be in a patient's best interests, or to maintain a treatment which is not proving helpful. Such a withdrawal of therapy may be assumed by others to be damaging, but it is not. (The writer has several times withdrawn antibiotics from elderly patients with pneumonia, only to see them improve.)

Euthanasia means to die gently, easily or fittingly; it is death with comfort and with dignity. This is something we might all wish for ourselves, as for all patients. But the word has been purloined so as to imply a contrived or induced death with those same properties of comfort and dignity (assuming, of course, that such is a possibility), whether that death is induced at a patient's request ('voluntary euthanasia') or not ('involuntary euthanasia'). Without doubt, any such euthanasia proposals would be, from the logical standpoint, within the realm of medical 'treatment', so it seems important to look at them against each of the ten aspects of medicinal therapy just detailed.

Several general points can be made from all that has been said. First, the possible *medical* grounds for euthanasia have changed. Until some forty years ago there might seem to have been considerable medical grounds for euthanasia; it was common for people to die lengthily, in great pain and physical suffering. Pain–relieving drugs were largely morphine and its immediate chemical cousins, and many doctors and nurses refused to use these, even in severe suffering, because it was imagined that problems of drug dependence and of 'medical ethics' forbade such use. With the return of hospice–type care, plus a number of new ways to relieve severe pain, the ground of physical suffering has largely disappeared. This is admitted even by some proponents of euthanasia (*e.g.*, the Dutch physician, Dr Admiraal, 1985). Since hospice care is discussed at length elsewhere in this symposium, no more will be said about it here.

The grounds for euthanasia are now really two, as argued by its proponents:

1. The avoidance of misplaced or meddlesome medicine aimed at cure, in patients who are likely to be far beyond such help and whose need is for care whilst they die naturally.

This is a protest against unjustified medical activity, which seems right on grounds of good medicine quite apart from moral or ethical considerations. However, to reassure patients that they can be defended against such needless medicine, the concept of the 'living will' has been introduced. In this concept, patients signify in writing, in advance of severe illness, that should they enter certain specified clinical states they would not wish to receive treatment aimed to conserve life. This notion is stated to be 'within the law', and in some countries there is already provision to proceed legally against a doctor who ignores a 'living will' (Voluntary Euthanasia Society, undated paper, *Some Questions Answered*).

2. Patients with incurable disabilities of body and or mind, who wish to die on grounds of mental suffering such as feelings of indignity, diminished capacity, burdensomeness to others and uselessness, can be assisted to commit suicide by a doctor who provides their means to this end.

How do these two situations relate to the general description of medicinal therapy given above?

First, several general conclusions follow from that description; therapeutic decision-making is a very complex and detailed matter; it is not a matter of routines. It should therefore best be left to those who care for the patient at the material time; it cannot be subjected to legal regulation or interference.

The next point is that though much turns upon patients' feelings about their situation, these feelings depend much upon their level of understanding of their problems, or upon bystanders' impressions of their suffering or wishes for them. However, patients' attitudes are not irreducible surds; the modern fashion to shape decisions solely upon a patient's wishes (complete autonomy) fails to take into account that these wishes are shaped by their relationships with others (or lack of them), by the information they have understood, and so on. In the play *Whose life is it anyway?*, by Brian Clark (1978), the last line spoken by the doctor to the disabled man who desperately demands euthanasia is, 'you might change your mind!'. This is clearly intended to evoke the reaction that the doctor is intransigent, insensitive and stupid. But, even if that patient was most unlikely to change his mind, the play neglects to point out not only that some patients *do* change their minds (*e.g.*, Vere, 1979), but more importantly that the patient's state of mind is now often accepted uncritically, as if it could never have been different. Yet every experienced doctor or nurse knows that very few patients retain such unchanging views, and if they do they are usually determined by past adverse experiences. The great majority of those who attempt suicide unsuccessfully never repeat the attempt (British Medical Association, 1988). Most importantly, the second ground for euthanasia (which was that of the patient in the play) is not a *medical* matter. It is a patient's wish for suicide, which cannot be carried into effect without medical help. Such situations should not be regarded as within the ambit of medicinal therapy. Patients have many wishes which doctors need feel no obligation to effect. The problem with the second proposed ground for euthanasia is that medical care stands in the way of it, yet medical procedures would be needed to effect it. Neither ground constitutes it a part of medicine.

What then of the first suggested ground, the 'living will'? It is indeed reasonable and right to protest against that meddlesome medicine that forces hopeless attempts to cure upon those whose only need is care whilst dying. But the problem with 'living wills' is that when they are made, there is no way in which a patient can anticipate the real circumstances which may surround subsequent illness

(Christian Medical Fellowship, 1988). An actual case illustrates the problem: a man with a hazardous cardiac rhythm disturbance suffered several episodes of cardiac arrest. During each of these he was resuscitated by electro shock and drug treatment. After six such episodes he said that the illness and its treatment were so distressing that should he arrest again, he would not wish to be resuscitated. He did arrest again whilst in hospital, as a registrar who did not know of his request was passing his bed. This doctor resuscitated the patient. Two years later the patient was back at work, with no recurrence of his illness and able to support his family. Had the registrar known of his expressed wish, things could have ended very differently; but no-one would have realised that an incorrigible, disastrous mistake had been made. This is no doubt a 'hard case', but many illnesses entail similar uncertainties of outlook, which a legally threatening 'living will' would overstep, irretrievably. It is, for example, often said that a 'living will' can be withdrawn should a patient change his or her mind. If the illness involves temporary confusion or unconsciousness there would not be that opportunity. The 'living will' concept is an exercise in idealism; it ill matches the practical realities of illness, and commits people to a course of action in advance of the facts, much to their own potential danger in some circumstances.

The key argument advanced by Admiraal (1985), one of the doctors who now practises officially accepted euthanasia in Holland, is that the doctor must remain the patient's ally right to the end. Hence, if euthanasia is that patient's sustained wish, it is right for the medical attendant to provide it. It is precisely at this point in medical ethics that a different view can and must be put: to argue thus is to raise autonomy to an overriding place and to neglect several other aspects of this complex problem. Even if deontology, or argument from general principles, is neglected it is never acceptable to argue that some degree of paternalism (decision of what is right over and against a patient's wishes) should not operate in tension with that patient's autonomy. The case just given of the man who wished not to be resuscitated is a stark example. It was best for him that he was resuscitated, as he later acknowledged; yet no-one could have foreseen the outcome. In the more frequent situation of the bitter, disabled person who feels useless and burdensome to others, it must be questioned whether there is or can be any state of essential uselessness or burdensomeness. Clearly, there is not. It is the patients' perception of themselves that seems an intense reality to them. That such situations can change is the message, and reality, of hospice care.

It is often assumed that severely disabled people, even if not in pain, wish that their lives might end. But the general truth is that this is a conclusion of those who observe them, not of the disabled themselves, who almost invariably value the only life they have ever known. They may seem 'pitiable objects', but seldom see themselves as pitiable subjects.

Hence euthanasia is acquiescence in hopelessness, the acceptance of despair. Medicine does not approach other problems like that; that would be basically foreign to the whole ethos of medicine, and has no necessary validity. Even if it be argued that a bad outcome is the fact in most patients with some defined disease, X, this never justifies the attitude that all sufferers from X should not be treated. Sufferers from X who do improve when treated justify the attempt to treat all, and that is the normal expectation from medical practice. Any different social expectation from medicine would alter doctor-patient relationships radically. If these were entered upon with the expectation that the doctor might serve as executioner, the practice of medicine in trust would not be possible. This would be true even were the patient someone who might accept euthanasia in principle.

Admiraal's stated principles for euthanasia follow:

1. It must exist within a formed doctor-patient relationship. The doctor must be the patient's ally.

2. Every possible human attention to relieve suffering must have been used.

3. The decision must be publicised, in the sense of being shared with medical peers.

4. It must be the patient's sustained wish.

5. It must be effected quickly.

It must be 'a deliberate life-shortening act, or the deliberate omission of a life-lengthening act in respect of an incurable patient in such a patient's interest'. Yet as has just been shown, this appealingly simple statement begs real questions at many points. The terms 'incurable' and 'patient's interest' carry questionable loads and do not bear careful scrutiny.

So far no discussion has been made of a more frequent medical problem, the case where to relieve suffering is to hazard life or limb to some degree. It has been shown that any therapy can be hazardous, and that the outcome must always remain in some degree uncertain. The problem of gaining relief at the cost of risk is somewhat different; there are cases where there is reason to anticipate that harm may come from therapy. For example, there is the patient (perhaps a smoker) with advanced cancer in lungs already damaged by severe bronchitis and emphysema. To relieve this person's pain with opiates may risk the depression of his breathing in a way that would not happen at the same doses in someone without lung disease. What should a doctor do? In this situation there is a very clear conflict between principles - the aim not to damage life and the aim to relieve suffering. Many, probably most doctors resolve this conflict by recourse to a heirarchy of ethical principles; if suffering is so intense that life cannot effectively be regarded as such by reason of its distressing quality and the impossibility of any normal function, then the aim to relieve suffering takes precedence over the aim to conserve life - to reverse this priority would sacrifice the ground so gained. However, it may be argued that this *is* euthanasia, and involuntary at that. If then euthanasia can be admitted here, why not in much wider contexts? Some ethicists, notably Roman Catholics, apply a 'doctrine of double effect' to such situations. It was not the intention to kill, only to relieve suffering. Others are unconvinced by this; if one acts to relieve suffering knowing that in so doing loss of life is likely, it is a small excuse that one did not intend what one could well foresee. A more secure logic would seem to be that no other course than to relieve such pain is practicable, that every treatment involves risk and that the more severe the problem the greater risk seems acceptable in relation to it. That at least is the general attitude in medicine. It seems important to recognise that the argument that allows hazardous relief of suffering where the quality of life is zero does not in and of itself invoke quality of life as an equally weighty matter in decisions where the degree of suffering is much less. It certainly enters the choice, but to a lesser degree. It is also important to recognise that when hazardous methods of relief are used they do not necessarily harm more than a minority of patients. Many patients gaining full pain relief improve, becoming able to function again and to relate to others.

From what has been said we can therefore draw several conclusions.

1. The situations of clinical choice are complex, and differ from case to case, and from time to time within one patient's illness. These decisions must therefore be left to local choice; general rules cannot be fairly applied, including those of laws allowing euthanasia or of 'living wills' applied *post hoc*.

2. 'Passive euthanasia', as often used to imply the withdrawal of therapy, is a misleading concept; there are many situations where it is right to withdraw treatment without intending to harm life. Harming life is the essence of euthanasia.

3. Voluntary euthanasia poses practical problems of the most severe and unacceptable kind. These include the fact that patients' wishes change, the perceived roles of health care professionals in patient care, the pressures that the possibility would bring upon the sick, the uncertain prognosis of many diseases, and the incorrigible nature of the euthanasia process itself. Above all, there is the fact that in modern medicine the apparent 'need' for euthanasia is virtually never for medical indication; medicine is involved simply because it stands in the way of suicide, yet could provide a ready means to achieve it.

It will be seen that in this paper only medical arguments have been discussed; this was its remit. This in no way implies that moral and ethical arguments are inapplicable, nor is it intended to exclude the import of clear doctrines in the Jewish-Christian traditions and biblical revelations about these problems. They are the subjects of other papers, as are the achievements of hospice care and other means to relieve terminal illness.

References

Pieter Admiraal, *Active Voluntary Euthanasia*, Voluntary Euthanasia Society (1985).

Sir Austin Bradford Hill, (1965) *Proc. Roy. Soc. Medicine*, 58, 295.

British Medical Association, *Euthanasia*, Report of the Working Party (1988).

Christian Medical Fellowship, 'Submission to the Chairman of the Working Party on Euthanasia', *C.M.F. Journal*, 34.1 (1988), pp. 21-24.

Brian Clarke, *Whose Life Is It Anyway?* Samuel French, London, (1978).

D. W. Vere, *Voluntary Euthanasia, Is There an Alternative?* Christian Medical Fellowship, London, (1971), revised and extended, 1979.

Voluntary Euthanasia Society, *Some Questions Answered*, undated paper, p. 1, para. 2.

Appendix

Some sections of the BMA Working Party report on Euthanasia (1988) are directly relevant to this paper and are stated elegantly and carefully. These are:

Section 6 (autonomy) The patient is regarded as authorising therapy, but cannot require a doctor to collaborate in their death.

7, 8, 9, 10. Compassionate life-ending in accidents, disasters, war is not comparable with ordinary medical practice. Disability involves the need for carers to reaffirm the value of the person, even when this seems lost to the sufferer; for infants the doctors' duty may be to ease dying, but not to end life actively, which would 'herald a serious and incalculable change in the present ethos of medicine'.

13. 'Living wills' are not yet recognised as binding in English or Scottish law. They require respectful attention and sensitive interpretation.

9

Recent Ethical Statements on Euthanasia: a Physician's Perspective

Anthony M. Smith

1. Background to the BMA Report

Where does the doctor go for ethical guidance in matters relating to death and dying, and euthanasia? Some may go to their own religious or philosophical system's teachers or writers - whether Christian or other religion, or humanist; and whether theirs by upbringing or persuasion. Some may rely on their innate feelings of what is wisest or best. Doctors have felt there was need of an accepted ethical standard acceptable to the majority of the profession and from a sufficiently authoritative source.

In 1977 the Annual Representative Meeting of the British Medical Association had affirmed that:

the position of medical practitioners who are in conscience opposed to euthanasia must be fully protected in future legislation should it occur, and that no legal obligation in this respect should be allowed to be imposed unilaterally on any member of the profession at any time.

But during the succeeding years public opinion is thought to have shifted, and there has been an urging that the position regarding euthanasia be reviewed.

In 1986 the Annual Representative Meeting of the BMA (representing 80% of Britain's medical practitioners - hospital doctors and General Practitioners, in both training and career grades) asked that the Association reconsider its policy (not implying that there was anything necessarily wrong with what doctors were doing, or with the BMA's advice, but rather urging the need for a fresh and critical examination of the policy). The ARM set up a Working Party to examine the questions around euthanasia and to report. The Working Party was led by the recently retired Chief Medical Officer, Sir Henry Yellowlees, and comprised a consultant paediatrician (Dr T. L. Chambers), a director of community medicine (Dr J. S. Horner), a general practitioner (Dr R. A. Keable-Elliott), a doctor-ethicist (Dr A. W. Macara), a geriatrician (Professor M. S. J. Pathy) and a hospice director (Dr. T. West). It was attended by - as observers - a solicitor and former chief nursing officer (Ms Mary Armstrong), a Queen's Counsel (Mr D. Sullivan) and a philosopher-neurosurgeon (Dr Grant Gillett).

It met fifteen times, received and examined sixty reports and written submissions, solicited opinion from interested individuals and groups and examined attitudes to the practice of euthanasia in other countries of Europe and farther afield. All this discussion led to a careful and authoritative Report which was received and debated by

Council of the BMA in May 1988, and has been published as *The Association's Advice on Euthanasia.* [1]

2. Scope and Basic Considerations of the Report
The Report begins by defining five terms used in these discussions:

> *Active Euthanasia* is usually taken to be an action performed within a medical setting which is done with the intention of terminating a human life. In the report we shall use the phrase 'an active intervention by a doctor to end life.'

> *Passive Euthanasia* tends to be used to describe the withdrawal or with-holding of some necessary treatment for the maintenance of human life. We shall use the phrase 'a decision not to prolong life' or 'a non-treatment decision.'

The Report states that these terms are used rather loosely and they prefer to use more precise words when discussing specific actions or decisions by doctors.

The remaining three terms produce more clear-cut ethical issues:

> *Voluntary' Euthanasia* is a death brought about by an agent *at the request of the person* who dies.

> *'Involuntary' Euthanasia* is the killing of someone who could consent but does not. Such an action is indistinguishable from criminal homicide and the claim that the motive for the killing is 'the best interests' of the victim is irrelevant.

---

1 *Euthanasia,* BMA Report.

'Non-voluntary' Euthanasia is the killing of an individual who has no capacity to understand what is involved, again out of kindness or a paternal consideration of the patient's 'best interests'. [paras 2-5.3]

The Report tries to hold in tension the ability of medicine to intervene and prolong life and the patient's autonomy, *i.e.*, his right to decide about what shall and shall not be done to him, to accede to or refuse advised treatment. It notes the increasing fear of many patients regarding loss of personality in the medical technology accompanying a prolonged dying. It notes the necessity of careful ethical thought as a basis for medical decisions affecting life and death - rather than *ad hoc* spur-of-the-moment decisions. And it declares that it is a basic truth that human life is of great value and should be cherished. [paras 7-11]

The Report tackles carefully many areas of difficult decisions, notably the incurably and painfully dying, the chronic incurably ill, the elderly confused patient (so-called 'senile'), the AIDS victim, the severely disabled (especially young persons), and the deformed or severely handicapped neonate. It covers also the person in the persistent vegetative state (commonly following a road accident, where the cortex of the brain has been extensively destroyed and one is left with persistent human life in which only certain reflex and automatic responses are left, and where there is no further hope of return to sentience), and the patient or person fearful of what his condition might one day become.

3. Personal Reflections on the Report

As a hospice doctor I deal constantly with patients with advanced cancer who are referred to us because of severe symptoms such as pain, nausea and vomiting, and so on. Earlier, as an orthopaedic associate specialist, I was concerned in the treatment of young acutely disabled people. In paediatric and obstetric junior hospital appointments - and latterly as an 'orthopod' - I was aware of problems surrounding the severely handicapped and deformed neonates and the pressures subsequently on the families of such children. Abroad in missionary service, particularly in single-handed missionary doctor situations, I knew about limited resources and the need to choose where such resources could and should be used.

In all these areas, what I read in the Report accords with my experience. I would like to share of few of these experiences with you to illuminate various findings of the Report.

A. The Patient with Advanced Cancer

In my first house job I remember vividly caring for an entertainer, a jolly man, suffering from pain arising from advanced cancer. Though it must be twenty-six years ago I remember clearly how that man suffered from desperate pain through weeks - perhaps two months - while we ran tests to try to find the cause, and while we failed to control his pain. I knew little about pain control, my chief seemed to know little more; we used what medication we dared to but his pain was never controlled: how could it be, on the doses of pain killers we were then using? Oh, that I had known then what I know now about pain relief!

He contrasts so vividly with a 64-year-old stockbroker who came to us in the hospice a while ago. He had the same sort of condition, a Pancoast Tumour (variety of lung cancer) at the apex of the right lung. He had had operations, radiotherapy, pain-controlling nerve blocks and even operations on the nerve pathways. To control his pain he needed - among other medications - 800mgs of morphine twice a day. But with that he was not being killed or made into a zombie: no, he watched television, did *The Times* crossword each day, and conducted his stockbroking business from his bed or chair - until his 65th birthday and his retirement. Oh, how important was retiring properly for this gentleman! Three days later he died. He had achieved his retirement, completed his working life, and been enabled to do so by proper pain control - and then he died, naturally and appropriately. The Report emphasises that it *is* possible to control pain and to relieve other symptoms.

Dawn was another example. She came to us with advanced cancer of the rectum and anus, with extensive local disease and horrible ulceration. She was troubled by pain, foul odour, poor bowel control and bleeding. I asked her what she wanted to aim for (as I usually do). She wanted pain control so that she could continue a useful life, and the security of care in the hospice. 'And can I have the injection to end it all when I feel the time has come, please?' I told her that we would willingly control pain and other symptoms, that we would not prolong life uselessly, but would aim to make this period as useful as possible. But that we could not shorten life. She was with us for four months. Pain was relieved - she was on 400mgs of morphine every four hours, the odour was eradicated, bowel control returned, bleeding stopped. She occupied her days very fully, even when confined much of the time to bed, and organised care for her disabled husband. We never had requests for euthanasia, but one night she woke with a new and severe abdominal pain, caused by a new complication (an intestinal perforation). Pain was relieved with an injection, she slipped into coma and died a few hours later - pain-free, peacefully, and naturally.

Here is the Report's comment on patients' autonomy which I have illustrated with Dawn:

Patient autonomy is a crucial aspect of informed patient care. This is achieved most successfully where a trusting and open relationship between the doctor and patient allows participation in decisions about illness and its treatment. Doctors should regard patients as authorising treatment, and should respect those authorisations and any decison to withdraw consent. But autonomy works both ways. Patients have the right to decline treatment but do not have the right to demand treatment which the doctor cannot, in conscience, provide. An active intervention by a doctor to terminate a patient's life is just such a treatment. Patients cannot and should not be able to REQUIRE their doctors to collaborate in their death. If a patient does make such a request there should be a presumption that the doctor will not agree. [para 6 of Conclusions]

Most of our patients need much less morphine than these two examples I have given; indeed, I am surprised to see how little analgesic most patients actually need if fear is actually relieved. I remember the patient who was talking to me about his illness, and I confirmed what he had suspected and feared, but which his doctor had never talked to him about, that the diagnosis was cancer. 'What does cancer mean to you?' I asked. 'It means pain and more pain, until one day I explode in pain.' How great was his relief when I could tell him - truthfully - that many patients with advanced cancer never do have pain; that pain is always controllable, often completely, and that death - when it did come - would almost certainly be a peaceful sleeping away. As one patient said to me, 'If dying is like I've just seen her do (of the patient in the next bed) - just waking and sleeping, and waking and sleeping, and then just sleeping, I'm not afraid of it any more.'

But all this comes from communication, the importance of which is highlighted in the Report. It says:

More important than debate about the limits of autonomy is the need for doctors and everyone else who is involved in the care of the terminally ill, to communicate with their dying patients. Doctors need to be able to elicit the fears of dying patients and to discuss and answer those fears. They need to be able to discuss terminal care openly so that patients can see that they will not be abandoned and left helpless in the face of a terminal disease. Only if such communication and good treatment becomes the norm can society expect to dissipate the pressure to force doctors to do things that the medical profession should not accept. [para 7 of Conclusions]

When I hear the comment that hospice is the place where people go to die, I generally reply that, on the contrary, hospice is a place where people go to live - and that is very largely because of free communication. But that is possible in hospital wards and general practices too. Why not?

B. The Young Disabled Patient
Paragraph 9 of the Report's conclusions reads:

Requests from young and severely disabled patients for a doctor's intervention to end their life present one of the hardest problems in day-to-day care. Counselling is essential to reaffirm the value of the person, and to counter pressure which may be created by the feeling of being unloved and an embarrassment or inconvenience to those upon whom the patient is wholly dependent. The subtle and dynamic factors surrounding disability and the wish to die make any drastic change in the law unwise for this group of patients.

Some of you will have heard of Joni. Joni Eareckson was a lively, healthy young lady who dived into too shallow a bay of sea water, hit her head on the sand, broke her neck, and was instantly quadriplegic. Conscious, with her full mental faculties, she made no recovery from her quadriplegia despite intensive treatment. Nevertheless, paralysed from the neck down, she has developed an incredibly fulfilling existence. She writes:

> I am actually excited at these opportunities 'to suffer for His sake' if it means I can increase my capacity to praise God in the process. Maybe it sounds glib or irresponsible to say that. Yet I really do feel my paralysis is unimportant.
>
> Circumstances have been placed in my life for the purpose of cultivating my character and conforming me to reflect Christlike qualities.... [2]

I remember a young man in his mid-twenties admitted through the Accident Department in Taunton's East Reach Hospital. He had been involved in a car accident, had a broken dislocated cervical spine, and was quadriplegic (all four limbs paralysed). Stabilisation of the fracture-dislocation surgically and intensive therapy allowed some improvement in his left hand and arm only. He was transferred to Stoke Mandeville Hospital and then to the Royal Hospital and Home for Incurables. That was how he was - and we did not expect to hear much more. However, a few months later we heard that he was to be baptised by total immersion, having come to a new personal faith in God - from being a young man with no time for God before his accident. The next we heard was that he was engaged to a nurse at the hospital, and then our ward sister was invited to his marriage. He has still three paralysed limbs and one which is greatly limited in what he can do with it, but he is now living in his own flat with his wife and continues a worthwhile life despite his handicaps. He speaks of what he has learned from his accident - and how he has grown!

---

[2] J. Eareckson, *Joni*. Pickering & Inglis, p.207

C. The Severely Malformed Infant
The Report states:

> Any move towards liberalising the active termination
> of a severely malformed infant's life would herald a
> serious and incalculable change in the present ethos of
> medicine. Nevertheless, there are circumstances
> where the doctor may judge correctly that continuing to
> treat an infant is cruel and that the doctor should ease
> the baby's dying rather than prolong it by the
> insensitive use of medical technology.
>
> This kind of decision requires careful communication
> between doctor, parents, nursing staff and other care-
> givers. It is imperative that the doctor should start
> from a position which seeks to preserve and value life
> rather than, on occasion, to judge it as not worthwhile.
> It is important also to stress that withholding
> treatment does not preclude loving care for the dying
> infant. This will, of course, involve relieving the infant's
> distress. [paras 10-11 of Conclusions]

I have not the time, nor adequate experience, to add
illustrations to this statement, but it balances well care for
the infant and concern for the parents and the burden that
may have to be borne for the years to come. Yet it does
not demean the value of this human life.

4. The Two Principal Findings of the Report
The first central principle of the Report is that it is not
appropriate to insist on treatment and the prolonging of life
against the patient's wish. In other words, a decision to
withhold active treatment, in order that natural death may
occur unencumbered by further treatments, is appropriate
care if the patient so wishes.

The Report states:

A number of (other) therapies could be considered to be life-prolonging or sustaining including the prescription of steroids, renal dialysis, blood transfusion and bone marrow transplantation, radiotherapy, and the use of chemotherapy and antibiotics. Consent by the patient is the only basis on which these treatments can be given. In each case the decision to refuse further treatment constitutes a revocable wish, sometimes unconscious, to succumb to a disease process rather than a decision to die at a certain definite time. In withdrawing any of these treatments the doctor is not directly abetting an act of suicide but is complying with a refusal to authorise further medical treatment which may be intrusive in some instances. [para 85]

Again,

'In clinical practice there are many cases where it is right that a doctor should accede to a request not to prolong the life of a patient. Appropriate medical skills and techniques should be offered to patients when there is a good chance of providing an extension to life that will have the quality that the patient seeks. [para 5 of Conclusions]

Here, there is indicated the value of the 'living will'. The living will is a device whereby a person expresses his attitude towards prolongation of life, active and intensive resuscitation and prolonged medication in the event of his becoming unable to make his wishes known - perhaps due to loss of consciousness or paralysis of vocal apparatus or to mental deterioration, of a prolonged and incurable sort. Such declarations have no force in law, but do indicate a person's wish and should be taken into careful account when deciding treatment. The Report states:

Advance declarations... may be a valuable guide to the
wishes of a patient who can no longer participate in
clinical decisions, but should not be regarded as
immutable or legally binding prescriptions for medical
care. They require respectful attention and sensitive
interpretation. [para 13 of Conclusions]

A full chapter in the Report is devoted to this matter. Two
notes of caution require sounding. A decision taken by a
person in full vigour and health relating to future treatment
in hypothetical circumstances may appear to him very
different in later life, after a gentle decline into limited
activity and mental ability which may feel appropriate to
that individual. Similarly, the outcome of vigorous and
successful resuscitation may be a much better quality of
life than could have been anticipated. Secondly, 'suffering'
(like beauty) may be in the eye of the beholder -
especially if he is a close and caring relative.

    I remember an elderly diabetic gentleman being admitted
to the hospice with an advanced cancer. Pain was relieved,
nausea and vomiting were not a problem. He sat much of
the day in his chair in the bay window of the ward and
much enjoyed his (rather small) meals, now that his
twenty–five years of diabetic dietary restrictions could
appropriately be discarded. He called the lady who came
round with tea in the afternoon 'the cake lady', since cake
had always previously been forbidden. He drowsed a lot,
and conversation was limited, but we felt pleased with his
enjoyment of life. I was surprised, therefore, to encounter a
distressed son and daughter-in-law one Sunday in the
hospice, who asked whether Dad could not be put out of
his misery as he was suffering so much. We sought to
eludicate the nature of his suffering. No, he had no pain,
they agreed. No, nausea and vomiting were not a problem,
and, yes, they had noticed how he enjoyed the hospice
food. "So 'suffering'?" I asked. They thought awhile and
then said slowly, "I suppose actually it is we who are

patient should be treated with the utmost respect. The medical team would need very strong reasons to override such a wish. 'Medical decisons are complex and difficult and correspondingly almost impossible to make in advance of a situation arising. When a medical crisis arises the medical team cannot solely rely upon projected and hypothetical expressions of intent which may or may not show a full appreciation of the problem... [para 236]

Finally, the Report declares that the law should not be changed. I quote:

An active intervention by anybody to terminate another person's life should remain illegal. Neither doctors nor any other occupational group should be placed in a category which lessens their responsibility for their actions.

The law should not be changed and the deliberate taking of a human life should remain a crime. This rejection of a change in the law to permit doctors to intervene to end a person's life is not just a subordination of individual well-being to social policy. It is, instead, an affirmation of the supreme value of the individual, no matter how worthless and hopeless that individual may feel. [paras 4 and 16 of Conclusions]

This has been worked out in great detail throughout the Report.

I end with the plea that the Report be heard. If ever our hospices or hospitals become places where patients' lives are terminated, I believe prospective patients will enter them much more anxious and fearful about what their doctor is actually going to do to them. Medical care will then have started down a totally new road, which will lead very literally to destruction.

individual, no matter how worthless and hopeless that individual may feel. [paras 4 and 16 of Conclusions]

This has been worked out in great detail throughout the Report.

I end with the plea that the Report be heard. If ever our hospices or hospitals become places where patients' lives are terminated, I believe prospective patients will enter them much more anxious and fearful about what their doctor is actually going to do to them. Medical care will then have started down a totally new road, which will lead very literally to destruction.

10

Implications of Euthanasia for Medical and Nursing Staff

Sarah Whitfield

I am an advocate of the literal meaning of euthanasia, 'a good death', but I am opposed to the currently accepted meaning, that of the deliberate killing of a patient, at his or her request, to end suffering. My experience of nursing patients of all ages, dying of a wide variety of illnesses, is that we can *always* offer care, comfort and support to the natural end, rather than intervening prematurely to bring about death by fatal injection. I believe in the sanctity and dignity of life, and in the appropriate relief of suffering - whether it is physical, mental, emotional or spiritual - in order to enable people to live until they die.

I am going to talk about the general principles of medical and nursing care and how these could be greatly changed if euthanasia was legalised. I am then going to concentrate on the practical implications of euthanasia for staff working with patients in hospital or at home with a chronic illness, or cancer, or who are elderly. I shall give some individual examples of patients I have nursed over the years as staff nurse, sister and nursing officer to illustrate some of the points I shall be making. It is important to realise that if euthanasia were ever legalised, its application would be to individual people who are all unique and in different circumstances, families and social backgrounds.

General Principles
People who enter the health professions are invariably highly motivated and caring men and women who wish to make sick patients better, prevent illness and suffering and to care for patients and their families. They want to preserve life and to improve people's quality of life rather than to control death or bring it about it prematurely. This is supported by medical and nursing codes of practice as follows. The International Code of Medical Ethics (World Medical Association 1949, 1969, 1983) states that: 'A physician shall always bear in mind the obligation of preserving human life.' The U.K. Code of Conduct for Nurses (1984) states: 'Act always in such a way as to promote and safeguard the wellbeing and interests of patients/clients.' (Number 1). And also: 'Ensure that no action or omission on his/her part or within his/her sphere of influence is detrimental to the condition or safety of patients/clients.' (Number 2).

Last year both medical and nursing professional bodies made statements opposing euthanasia. The British Medical Association Working Party's Report on Euthanasia concluded that:

> The law should not be changed and the deliberate taking of a human life should remain a crime. This rejection of a change in the law to permit doctors to intervene to end a person's life is not just a subordination of individual wellbeing to social policy. It

is, instead, an affirmation of the supreme value of the individual, no matter how worthless and hopeless that individual may feel. [1]

The Royal College of Nursing's Nursing Forum on AIDS also issued a timely statement on euthanasia which reflects the general RCN policy as follows:

The RCN Nursing Forum on AIDS is vehemently opposed to any initiatives which would seek to legalise euthanasia for people with AIDS. Such legalised death would encourage the prevalent ignorance about the condition and decelerate the research being undertaken into this condition. It could also have serious ramifications for other chronically and terminally ill people. Rather medicine and nursing should grasp the opportunity to pursue education about this condition, and gain information and knowledge so that symptomatic manifestations of AIDS can be relieved, enabling people to live to the full the remainder of their lives, and eventually achieve an easy death without the need for euthanasia. [2]

The introduction of euthanasia would, therefore, be in direct opposition to both nursing and medical codes of practice and their professional bodies. Young people could think twice before applying to enter one of the health professions, if there was a change of emphasis from preserving life and promoting the wellbeing of patients to deliberately bringing about the death of a patient prematurely - however good the intention might be. The availability of euthanasia could undermine the traditional

---

[1] *Euthanasia*, BMA, 1988, p. 69, no. 16.

[2] 'No Final Solution' by Jamie Fleming, *Nursing Standard*, 25 June 1988, p.11.

respect for human life, and the practice of doctors and nurses could alter and take the 'easy way out', instead of looking for alternative treatments and care to relieve suffering, and support the patient and his family.

In both nursing and medicine, trusting relationships are built up between the patient and his doctor or nurse. This is particularly so in the community, where general practitioners may look after various members of a family over many years, and district nurses may visit the chronically ill at home regularly for the same period. In hospital, nurses are encouraged to get to know their patients as individuals, and in some wards a system called 'primary nursing' has been introduced where a named nurse follows the patient through from admission to discharge. Hospital consultants, particularly physicians and geriatricians, can have patients coming to see them over a number of years. All this means that doctors and nurses get to know their patients in many circumstances and patients trust them to prescribe appropriate treatment and to give care which sustains and promotes their quality of life. Would that same trust be there with the spectre of euthanasia in the background? Could professionals who really know their patients well administer a lethal dose of a drug to kill them prematurely? Would there not be an enormous sense of failure that they could not find a less radical way of relieving suffering? I consider that there would. Any professional acting in such a way would have to live with that on his or her conscience, and in the long term this could be destructive.

From the patient's point of view, if he was aware that euthanasia was legal, he might question much more what the doctor prescribed for him - and could fear going into hospital. Patients should not have to endure such worries and anxieties.

Nurses and doctors gain job satisfaction from the care that they give their patients and from valuing them as individuals and human beings. Anything which has the potential to devalue human life must be seriously questioned, and euthanasia has that potential. If human life starts to become worthless, some of that job satisfaction would go - it becomes the thin end of the wedge. *The introduction of euthanasia would represent a fundamental shift for doctors and nurses from preserving life to controlling death.* I believe that we should not make that shift.

Patients with a Chronic Illness

Chronic ill health takes many different forms, from slowly-worsening heart and/or lung disease, to arthritis in its various forms, and deteriorating conditions such as multiple sclerosis and motor neurone disease. The main burden of caring for these patients at home falls on relatives, friends and good neighbours - with regular, often daily, visits from the district nurse to help with lifting, personal hygiene and other nursing needs. The general practitioner may be a regular visitor too, or only called in when there is a medical crisis. Many patients have acute episodes of illness requiring admission to hospital for treatment, *e.g.* a chest infection which exacerbates already diseased lungs and causes severe breathlessness. It is often difficult to judge clinically when such an admission could be the patient's last, and when active treatment aimed at discharging him home turns to terminal care and support. I have known a number of such patients, some of whom have openly asked, "Do you think I will go home this time?" but none has asked to be put out of their suffering for ever. Some people might judge their lives to be of poor quality, since they are confined to the house and breathless, but they have a will to live, and nurses and doctors must always persevere to help them to live. If such a patient asked for euthanasia, the temptation would be for staff not to strive so hard, and to let them go. The result would be a questioning of whether the doctor was right and what the patient might have achieved if allowed his natural life span.

Other patients with deteriorating physical conditions come into hospital at planned intervals for respite care - to give their families a well-earned break. What would the situation be if some of these asked for euthanasia, motivated either by their own wish to die and to suffer no longer, or because they did not want to be a burden on their families?

I can think of two ladies in their fifties, both with multiple sclerosis which confines them to bed or a wheelchair. They are able to feed themselves but are dependent on others for every other aspect of daily living. I got to know them well as they came into my medical unit regularly for respite care. They have contrasting personalities. Rose is a dignified lady who takes a real pride in her appearance, and her voluntary helper comes in weekly, including during her hospital stays, to paint her nails and set her hair. She always wears pretty nighties and shawls. The other, Lily, is a true Eastender with a cockney accent and a good line in swearwords. She doesn't really care what she looks like, but she is warm–hearted, enjoys a flutter on the horses and her daily pint of Guinness and weekly carton of jellied eels. Both need full nursing care, but are favourites with the nurses. The houseman's involvement during their admission is usually minimal - a brief clerking when they first arrive, writing up the appropriate drug prescriptions and giving a short report on the consultant's round. He is too busy with other emergency admissions for anything else. Imagine this scenario then, when they both come the next time as planned admissions for respite care, but on this occasion circumstances have changed for each of them. Rose has been dependent on her husband for her care at home and they are devoted to each other, but her husband is finding

it more difficult to cope and recently had a hospital
admission himself for back strain. Rose does not want to
go into a nursing home or hospital permanently, but she
doesn't want to be a burden either. So she asks for
voluntary euthanasia, for the sake of her husband. On the
other hand Lily is having increasing urinary tract
infections, her skin is breaking down more easily into
pressure sores, and she can no longer feed herself. She
has had enough, and wants to be put out of her misery.
How would the staff react? The houseman is completely
taken aback - he is in the middle of his first house job,
keen, anxious to do his best for his patients, and here he is
faced with not two planned admissions for respite care, but
two patients wanting him to give them a fatal injection and
bring their lives to a premature end. It goes against all he
has been taught about preserving life and giving
appropriate treatment. Can he really stand by a patient's
bed and give an injection which will kill her? The nursing
staff are equally shocked. The sister and staff nurses know
and love Rose and Lily. They have already told the new
students about them and the challenges of nursing care
that they present. There must be an alternative to their
requests for euthanasia, but it needs time, patience,
listening quietly to each of them, and working out
appropriate solutions to the two seemingly insurmountable
problems. The nurses would not be able to stand by and
allow two well-liked patients to die prematurely because
they could not find the right solutions. The danger could be
that pressure on a very busy medical ward might tempt
staff to take the seemingly easy way out and give the fatal
injection. But how would they feel afterwards? I think they
would feel failures, because they did not find alternatives
which could have helped and supported Rose and Lily and
their families and thus preserved life and not cut it short. A
tremendous sense of guilt would live on in both the doctors
and the nurses, and the thought 'if only' would keep
recurring.

In fact, these situations did arise with both Rose and Lily; but without the specific request for euthanasia. In Rose's case she stayed in hospital longer than planned while special lifting apparatus was put in at home, and more voluntary and paid support organised through the Care Attendant's Scheme. With Lily, she needed a lot of time and support to help her feel valued and that her life was worth living, which nurses, the chaplain, the social worker and her own family gave her. A specialist in urinary tract infections was brought in to advise, and new pressure–relieving devices for her bed and chair were organized. All this took time and effort, but the end results were certainly worthwhile.

Patients with Cancer
The cancer ward which was part of my medical unit admits patients from all over the region at various stages of the disease. Some arrive for further investigations just after the diagnosis of cancer has been made and before a treatment regime is commenced. Others come in at regular intervals for chemotherapy and blood checks. Some return after a long interval with secondaries, and a number are with us in the terminal stages of their illness before a peaceful death. Sometimes there were conversations with patients about their wish not to suffer at the end, but they were always reassured that distressing symptoms could be, and would be, controlled. Because the same patients were in and out at regular intervals for treatment, the staff got to know them well. They saw them through various crises, not only to do with the illness but family ups and downs too. Staff nurses enjoyed the continuity of care that this pattern of admissions gave, and often stayed longer on the ward than on other general wards because of the increased job satisfaction. They were highly motivated, and were able to give care and support up to the end. If a patient came into this caring and often busy ward requesting euthanasia, how would the staff feel? Disappointed and upset, I think, that the patient needed

actually to ask for a premature ending to his life, when the staff were working hard to relieve distressing symptoms, offering support and care in a friendly atmosphere, and trying to meet individual needs. I think that the staff would seriously question what they were doing and how they could alter their care so that patients did not have to ask to die.

Another side to this is that there are always surprises - patients go into remission unexpectedly, they outlive their original prognosis by months and even years, they are able to fulfil ambitions they thought they would never achieve. Could we risk all of this by agreeing to euthanasia? A further aspect is that cancer treatment is always pushing the frontiers back, finding new and more effective drugs and other forms of therapy. If we gave up too soon on individuals, would we be less keen to continue research and look for different ways of treating people? The answer to requests for euthansia from cancer patients is high standards of terminal care - at home, in hospital or in a hospice.

The Elderly
The elderly are another group who fear being a burden on their families or other carers, and may feel that they should ask for euthanasia. We tend to forget that the majority of old people live in their own homes, sometimes with relatives, often on their own, and remain in good health and enjoying life for a number of years. However, as they grow older they do become more frail and dependent, and may eventually need continuing care - either from family at home, or in an elderly ward or nursing home. In hospital or nursing home it is the nurses who are with the patients twenty–four hours a day. Many Care of the Elderly units are difficult to staff, but where the senior nurses are innovative and provide professional leadership as in Tameside, the nursing unit in Burford, Oxford, and the professorial nursing ward in Manchester, there are fewer

recruitment problems. The care of the elderly is seen as a challenge, and as a means of giving skilled compassionate nursing care. Nurses get to know their elderly patients very well. Some can be cantankerous and difficult to manage, but there will always be at least one nurse, often the auxiliary, to whom they will respond.

If euthanasia were to be carried out with elderly patients who had requested it earlier in the form of a 'living will', who would make this decision, and on what grounds? When does an elderly person become so physically frail, or mentally confused, that it is appropriate to administer that fatal injection? The nurses who know them as individuals won't want to make the decision, I am sure. Should it be the geriatric consultant? But what does that say about his motivation in specialising in geriatric medicine, if he is then going to decide a premature end for his patients? Many nurses would find it difficult to nurse someone if they knew in advance the exact date and hour of his death. Nurses who work with the elderly are sad when they die, but at the moment these are natural deaths and they do not know the precise moment. The timing is in God's hands. The great risk of euthanasia is that it will diminish the worth of the frail and the demented. Why bother? They will be dead tomorrow. Surely this is unacceptable.

Let me share with you another example, Agnes, an old lady on the continuing care ward of a hospital. She is mentally alert but physically crippled with arthritis which confines her to bed or electric wheelchair. She has no close relatives. I used to see her on my evening and weekend rounds of the hospital, and we had the same conversation each time 'I want to be put away. There is no point in being alive. I am a nuisance to the nurses. I wish euthanasia were legal.' My reply was always the same: 'You know I can't "finish you off" and I wouldn't want to. You keep us all going with your quips and jokes. The nurses enjoy looking after you.' After a number of months she was transferred to the first NHS nursing home in the district. She has her own room, she likes the communal facilities and home rather than institutional cooking, and she is able to plan her own day rather than have it dictated by ward routine. She now enjoys living and no longer talks of euthanasia. Surely this is the better way to care.

Alzheimer's disease and senile dementia are conditions that many fit and capable people fear developing, and such fear may prompt them to sign a 'living will', an advance declaration of the wish for voluntary euthanasia. How would this work in practice? I can think of two men with Alzheimer's disease at different stages, being currently cared for at home by their wives. One is a doctor who had to take early retirement. His behaviour is now child-like, and he doesn't recognise his own grandchildren though he will reminisce happily about his medical student days. The other is a bank manager who also retired early, and he can at times be physically violent towards his wife whom he doesn't always know. Both wives are devoted to their husbands and want to keep them at home as long as possible. If these men had signed a 'living will', at what point would the doctor decide to carry out euthanasia? When they need hospitalisation? But what would that do to their wives who have looked after them? They could be forced into trying to cope for longer at home to prevent euthanasia being administered.

Practical Considerations

Finally, I would briefly like to consider the practical implications of administering euthanasia. Who would do it? The doctor responsible for the patient, or someone from another medical team? Or would it be delegated to the nurse? I would certainly strongly resist shifting the responsibility from the prescribing doctor to the allocated nurse. And how would pharmacists feel about dispensing a lethal drug intended to kill a patient?

If the doctor does administer the fatal dose, how does he view what he is doing? Is it the last act of kindness to the patient, or is it an admission of failure to control distressing symptoms - not make the patient feel a burden, or not to be able to provide an appropriate type of care for him? Surely it goes against all that the doctor stands for?

If euthanasia becomes acceptable, how will this affect nurses? Caring for the terminally ill is one of the most rewarding aspects of nursing provided that nurses are given adequate resources and support to help them. There is something almost sacred and very precious about being with a patient at the time of dying, knowing that it is in God's hands. Many times I have been with young student nurses at their first death, and it is a privilege and a responsibility. The timing of the actual end is never certain, which it would be with euthanasia. The caring goes on until the end and afterwards. Nurses can get distressed now if they give the last regular injection of diamorphine before the patient's death, because they feel they have brought about the death, which they certainly haven't. How would they feel if that is what actually happened after the doctor gave the fatal injection? It would undoubtedly alter our whole outlook on caring for the dying.

Conclusion
In conclusion, then, there are definite implications for doctors and nurses caring for patients if euthanasia were legalised. The trusting relationship between doctors and nurses and their patients would be at risk; there would be a change in emphasis from doing everything possible to relieve suffering to taking the so-called easy way out; the *raison d'etre* for people entering the health professions would be in question; and the worth of human life would be devalued. There are positive alternatives to euthanasia, and these should be pursued instead. Appropriate care and

support, relief of distressing symptoms and respect for the sanctity of life are better ways than euthanasia.

11

Euthanasia: the AIDS Dimension

Robert George

In being asked to speak about the AIDS dimension to euthanasia I am in somewhat of a dilemma. Those of you who have had contact with me will know that I am preoccupied with emphasising the similarities between palliative and terminal care of people with cancer and AIDS rather than looking at the differences. I am not alone, I hope, in the view that the principles and practice of palliative medicine are largely independent of the disease process leading to terminal illness. Having said that, I see it falling to me to look at the key arguments around euthanasia and apply them specifically to the distinctives, perceived or otherwise, that are frequently spoken of with respect to HIV–related disease. I shall treat the issues around euthanasia that I feel merit specific comment with respect to AIDS in an order of convenience rather than importance.

The Sanctity of Life World View

John Fletcher, a lawyer, says: 'The public's debate about the morality of euthanasia must not depend on the likelihood that all parties entertain what they believe to be an impossible and self–defeating conflict.' [1] Or as Dr Johnson may have said: 'It is not possible for neighbours in dispute to agree as they are arguing from different premises.' Within our pluralistic society today, and particularly with respect to AIDS, this is a truism. Fletcher goes on to say: 'It is certainly important in current debate that a person should not be required to adopt a theological viewpoint in order to assent to arguments.'

I agree wholeheartedly with that, and I see it as our responsibility to know the house we live in but to move across the road for meaningful debate to take place. However, on the subject of death and dying, it is naive *not* to acknowledge that *all* people have a spiritual perspective, even if that is the desolation and hopelessness of atheism or some moral code from they know not where.

So, without relying on the sanctity of life as my only argument against euthanasia, I feel it necessary and logical to set markers that point to why, with respect to AIDS at least, sanctity of life is neither a bedrock of care nor a common stand upon which to debate. In trying to convey the essence of this schism, without appearing trite or quasi–theological, I have found ringing in my ears the refrain of the closing chapters of Judges which is summed up in the last sentence of the book: 'In those days, Israel had no king: everyone did as he saw fit' (Judges 21 v 25). The refrain has been updated by Sartre: 'On a shattered and deserted stage without script,

---

[1] J.C.Fletcher, ch.22, p.297. *Controversies in Oncology.* Ed Petra, HIV., John Wiley, 1982.

director, prompter or audience, the actor is free to improvise his part'.

Relativism and situational ethics, self–determination and society's current, and unfortunately necessary, preoccupation with human rights in my opinion all come out of a lack of absolute. We need to admit within our hearts and churches that much of the responsibility for this is ours. Are we surprised that society looks upon the church and Christianity as 'an object of scorn and a byword amongst the nations where the people say, Where is their God?' (Joel 2 v 17)? Men and women I know relate how they have turned so often to an unhearing, uncaring, ignorant and prejudiced church in search of the personal God they need to help in their struggle with issues and tensions of addiction, personal identity or sexuality. To the outside world many of our congregations appear to have no communication with our Father in heaven. As a cartoon read recently: 'Every time I pray, all I seem to get is the ansafone.'

I saw that on the notice board of a secular, voluntary, caring organisation. That to me is a cry for help. Where there is no clear evidence of a king or a kingdom, what can people do other than what they think is right? The real problem with the inevitable situational ethics that result is that we can none of us be totally objective to the extent that we may not even be aware that self–interest, deception or delusion is operative. Fear, power and control are so often the emotions that are in the ascent.

We must accept that for many people with AIDS, making major decisions about control and authority within their lives has been an emotional and frequently a spiritual watershed. Individuals have had to confront, for example, the reality of choosing a lifestyle that will in all probability open them up to misunderstanding, prejudice and ostracism. For people who have made expensive decisions such as this in the control of their lives, the power and authority to die when they choose is a logical endpoint of that world view.

As those who have chosen to submit to the Lordship of Jesus, while being secure and immovable in our faith, we of all people should understand what choice really means. Regardless of how we feel, we need to be aware of it and understand and attempt to relate to those who live on fundamentally different premises. I echo Dame Cicely Saunders in that it is for this reason if no other that any debate on euthanasia must stand or fall on issues unrelated to sanctity of life. Whilst this cuts right across the grain for those of us who see life as a gift from God during which we are meant to learn to relate to him, it is a rock upon which many do not wish to stand. I do not wish to address any more of the issues of choices, power and control as there are many far more able to do this than I - besides, I am switching into preacher mode.

Definitions and Semantics

What I have just said ties in with semantics and definitions. The issue of definitions is very much open to question in the whole area of AIDS, and I think this again represents the fluxes and relativism that are endemic in our society. Hence there is a clear lack of distinction between voluntary euthanasia, passive euthanasia and palliative care. I am sure no one here would have trouble in making clear distinctions and I would hope that the use of the term 'passive euthanasia' would fall outside most people's vocabulary. If I may just define what I mean by euthanasia, then — it means an active or direct means to end the life of a dying person who requests another to terminate his or her life in the name of mercy.[2]

---

[2] J.C.Fletcher. Is Euthanasia ever justifiable? pp.297-321. *Moral Policy on Euthanasia.*

Let me give an example. Only two days ago, a person on receiving the news of his imminent deterioration said: Why can't it be finished today? When asked why, he retorted that he was in terrible pain (ten minutes before he denied all symptoms of pain). When I reassured him that the pain was not a problem to control, his immediate reply was 'Oh that's OK then isn't it?' He complained no more.

I relate this because it illustrates not only the reality and acute potential of emotional and spiritual pain, but more particularly the confusion between good symptom control and what a proselytist would claim as a request for euthanasia.

My refrain today is: 'The only realistic way forward in providing a robust alternative to euthanasia is a widespread practice of high quality palliative medicine and its incorporation into the standard undergraduate curriculum.'

The Opinions of Patients - Who Wants Euthanasia?

As time goes by I am increasingly aware that all swords have two edges - certainly within the arena of AIDS.The first is the benefit and challenge of looking after this client group which is young, extremely well informed, intelligent, articulate and vocal. This has allowed us in care provision to make rapid and significant moves in both therapy and practical provision because of cooperation and political activity. But on the other hand, perhaps for the first time in its life, the medical profession in the broadest sense of the word has been directly under scrutiny and audit by its client group. This sits uneasily with the unwritten status that we so easily adopt. We doctors find it difficult to be confronted, challenged or corrected by our patients. Personally, I welcome this freedom of dialogue and audit, although there are many who do not. Kennedy in the *Management of Terminal*

Malignant Disease says 'The particularly intractible problem which bedevils all medico–legal discussions and is highlighted in the care of the terminally ill (is) the tension between the paternalism of the doctor and society and the right to self-determination of the patient'.

The issue of a patient's control over his care has of course been resolved in palliative medicine where we are familiar with letting go of what we feel is best in deference to what the patient feels is best.   Not surprisingly, then, my immediate response in being asked to speak at this conference was to enter into phrenetic and unstructured attempts to get opinions from people with HIV infection and AIDS - two quite separate groups, incidentally, as to their views on euthanasia. How naive of me!

However, ethics committee willing, it has stimulated me into planned cooperation with the consumer organisations to try and examine this area in a comprehensive and definitive way.   Whilst I am tempted to use preliminary information, I think that that would cause me to fall foul of the criticism that I am about to direct at those who have spoken thus far in the media on the subject of euthanasia and AIDS.

I will therefore confine my comments to the experience of care of some 110 patients in the last year.   The data I will mention come both from my experience running palliative medicine services for people with AIDS in Bloomsbury and the Middlesex Hospital and also my contact with the Mildmay Mission Hospital's Continuing Care Unit for people with AIDS, and I wish to acknowledge the work and skills of the staff in both teams.

Certain sections of the media and proponents of euthanasia would lead us to believe that a significant proportion, if not indeed the majority of people with HIV or HIV-related disease, want seriously to consider euthanasia as a caring and 'therapeutic' option. I find no evidence of this in tangible form within the world literature and it is certainly not borne out by my experience. Loose statements such as 'over half of the friends that I have would have euthanasia if it was available' are simply not sufficient to persuade anyone. Equally, the interview of a number of people wishing or planning euthanasia is just as insubstantial.

As of April 1989 there are no data in the world press on euthanasia in connection with HIV infection either in terms of incidents or wishes of the client group.

Our personal experience of care is important for two reasons. Firstly, death and dying are addressed specifically as part of care, both with family or carers. Within our care planning, symptom control, *modus mortis*, suicide, euthanasia and so on are discussed with all patients.

Subsequently we have certainly addressed the subject in significant terms with approximately 10% of people, and less than 2% of patients under our care have pursued euthanasia vigorously as a realistic option. In one patient, this issue has not been resolved as the subject has only just arisen, but interestingly, in the other patient, the offer of contact with the Voluntary Euthanasia Society has not been pursued and furthermore, following a stay in hospice, he has dispensed with euthanasia altogether. In our experience therefore, certainly amongst those in the last month of their life, euthanasia is a serious option in only a small minority, and in our experience this is symptomatic of an unresolved agenda, rather than a considered and clear choice. This is of course in the face of what we would consider to be good and appropriate palliative medical care - and again I will give you my refrain: the only realistic way forward in providing a robust alternative to euthanasia is a widespread practice of high quality palliative medicine and its incorporation into the standard undergraduate curriculum.

Why is there this disparity between genuinely held yet unsubstantiated opinion on the incidence of the desire for euthanasia and the statistics that we seem to be accumulating? Well, all informed people should know by now that the testing of a person as HIV antibody positive, whilst indicative of a viral infection, is by no means synonymous with AIDS or terminal disease, and at the moment we are not even sure that all people with HIV infection will progress to full blown AIDS.

Having said this, the state of medical knowledge is such in 1989 that people with HIV infection cannot be cured, and epidemiological data suggest that the majority will ultimately develop AIDS or disease related to HIV with the passage of years or even decades. It is therefore very much on the agenda of everyone infected that they may be facing a life shortened by illness whilst at the same time attempting to live positively with it. As we all know, the spectre of death, particularly in those with unresolved psychological or spiritual needs is frequently far worse than the reality, and I am interested to see that those speaking of euthanasia are by and large living with the disease and functioning productively. My suspicion is that as many approach death and dying and are cared for and counselled appropriately, the resolution of conflict within self and world view(I define this as a person's perception of reality and the world and the way he fits into it) will lead to a desire to experience and go through the full process of dying rather than to amputate or terminate the last weeks or months of life. Do I have evidence to support this rather stark statement? Well I think I do. Retrospective data on those committing suicide - in New York in the mid-1980's, I must add (and therefore not in any sense directly applicable to the English experience) - suggest that suicide is some 36 fold higher amongst people with HIV infection than in the general population, and significantly greater than amongst people with other chronic diseases.[3] Interestingly, these deaths appear to have been among relatively healthy people and seem related temporally to the receipt of diagnosis rather than the onset of intolerable symptoms.

Experience from our work shows that people with significant pathology are far more interested in acute medical intervention (what I call therapeutic mentality) than in ways of ending their life. We have also found that some 50% of our patients have a significant change in attitude and world view in the last three months of their life, moving from the desire for acute intervention and the delaying of death towards acceptance and spiritual and emotional peace.   The introduction of voluntary euthanasia means, therefore, that many people will be denying themselves this crucial time when half of them are likely to have major shifts in their emotional and spiritual attitude. This dramatic move in world view is by no means confined to the emotionally labile. Let me give two examples. 'You must die intelligently, the way you would sell a position you were defending. . . make it the most expensive position ever sold' (Ernest Hemingway). Here you see on the one hand the predictable intransigence of one famous atheist who fulfilled the criterion of intellectual honesty by destroying himself in the hallway of his home with his favourite shotgun; and on the other the dawning of potentially the most significant U-turn in twentieth century intellectual life: (Looking back) 'I find it difficult to conceive that there is

---

[3] P.M.Marzuk, H.Tierney, K.Tardiff *et al.* 'Increased risk of suicide in persons with AIDS'.
J.Am.Med. Ass. (1988) 259–90, 1333-1337.

not more to life than this' (Sartre in the last weeks of his life). Better that - I shudder to think how many may be tempted to stop living before their appointed time and thereby deny themselves the possibility of personal integration or faith because euthanasia was available.

I would add here, also, a direct challenge to the statements made by Dr Admiraal who was recently on television (Heart of the Matter, 26 February 1989, produced by Joan Bakewell, BBC), that the opportunity for euthanasia in the last weeks and days of life is important. We have learnt, always to our delight, and sometimes also to our embarrassment, that prognostication and AIDS are two words that do not go together. On the one hand, up to 25% of deaths may be unexpected, and in every case that we have encountered, unwelcomed by the patient; on the other hand the number of patients accepted for palliative medical care, with expected survivals of less than one month who have, with good symptom control and counselling, been able to extend both the quantity and quality of their life by several months, now runs well into double figures.

Of the forty-seven deaths with the Bloomsbury Community Care Team, two have been due to suicide. One was by a bereaved lover who incidentally also had AIDS, where the patient took his life two weeks after the death of his partner. The second occurred on the day of referral so it is not possible to make comments upon the factors of importance. One patient who has attempted to take his own life now sees suicide and euthanasia unfavourably following appropriate care within a hospice setting. With the information I have thus far, therefore, I am quite comfortable flying in the face of apparent public opinion on the desire of people with AIDS to consider euthanasia.

Finally, I would say that the main representative body of people with AIDS and AIDS–related illnesses, Frontliners, was heard on the recent television programme on euthanasia to come out very much in favour of life, while acknowledging a person's right to end his or her life. They have a policy not to discuss euthanasia publicly.

The Process of Dying

Before making some emotive statements which are nevertheless in my opinion valid, I would like to start with a statistic. On average we care for people in the last 2-3 months of their life, and 50% of them have a major change in world view during that period of time. This is in no sense the result of proselytism, but is a natural consequence of individuals addressing the fundamentals of being both human and spiritual beings.

Those of us with faith and a belief in the existence of heaven would see the natural process of dying as being very much part of our movement from life to life and in that critical stage, if you like, we are flipping between parallel realities. Any absolute intervention into the timescales of movement would be in my opinion and world view, blasphemous. Those of us working with the dying will, without exception I am sure, agree that the period of an individual's life at this time is particularly poignant, precious and private. We have all seen the dealings of God with man even when a patient is slipping in and out of consciousness, or is frankly comatose, and I for one dare not interfere in that process. What is the consequence of an individual having once made a statement of desire for euthanasia if the time comes when he is no longer available for comment and he no longer wishes euthanasia to take place? What are the psychological and spiritual dynamics involved? No one can answer.

What of the person who has elected to take a fatal draught of drug? According to the statements of Dr Admiraal on television recently, the period of time from taking the draught to death may be of the order of six hours. What happens in the mind and spirit of the person as they sit within this irreversible and self-administered or self-determined time? No one knows. Are we sure that the quality of death is good and painless? No one knows. I will come back to these three points later.

What of the stories of individuals being awake and aware throughout operations where anaesthesia is supposed to have been adequate and complete? Many tell of the respiratory distress of being paralysed by curare and waiting for the next tidal breath from their ventilator. What, I wonder, is the effect upon somebody partially anaesthetised and curarised whose respiratory failure is not because of central nervous system depression but muscle paralysis? We cannot be sure that consciousness has been ablated in every individual.

I seriously question the assurance that euthanasia is a good quality death because of these unanswerable questions.

We are all agreed that HIV is a new disease and, not surprisingly, the level of medical endeavour has been both enormous and possibly unique in the extent and significance of the strides that have been taken in managing both the components of AIDS and specifically in scientists' attempts to overcome the activities of the virus within the body. However, as we all know *pari passu* with this, the issues of symptom control and the place of the patient at the centre of therapeutic strategy has been paid at best lip service as people have been unwilling to move to a palliative strategy. There is no doubt in my mind that much of the suffering and anguish, particularly on approaching death, has been to a greater or lesser degree as a result of this preoccupation with cure, albeit motivated by a desire to overcome and help. Many would quote the advances in cancer care as having required this level of commitment to therapeutic intervention, and I acknowledge that tension, although it does not change my opinion. There is, however, an additional dimension, and that has been the unwillingness of the hospice movement to take on board the needs of this new group of dying people.

I do not say that in order to accuse, but there is absolutely no doubt that the best in symptom control and palliative medicine has been denied these people for these two reasons up until the beginning of 1988 when the Mildmay provided the first dedicated hospice facility for people with AIDS in Europe, and in that period of time specific terminal care services were developed both at St Mary's and by our team at the Middlesex.

It is not surprising, therefore, that people who have seen friends, partners and lovers die uncomfortable and emotionally painful deaths, should say that medicine has failed them - indeed it has; not by lack of expertise but by our failure to address the need for palliative medical care of the highest standard. Whilst I would admit that is part of the evolutionary process of this new area, it has provided significant ammunition for those seeking euthanasia as a therapeutic option. I am delighted to say that commitment within the hospice movement is now high towards learning and applying principles of palliative medicine to this group, and excellent courses and opportunities are now available for people to be trained to apply their expertise.

At the end of the day, arguments against euthanasia have absolutely no credibility unless they are backed up by the highest standard of palliative medical care which is available to all sectors of society. I repeat my refrain. It seems to me mandatory and urgent that every district general hospital should be able to refer to a palliative physician and an appropriate terminal care service. In this respect, of course, the establishment of palliative medicine as a recognised sub–speciality for higher medical training is both timely and welcome.

The Needs of Carers

In keeping with the experiences of people working with cancer deaths, the most significant contributor to patients' admission at the end of their lives are the additional psychosocial needs of those caring for them at home. For many, this is the financial pressure of being the breadwinner, but also many carers have been bereaved on several occasions or are themselves coping with HIV infection. For many there is a deep sense of failure that their friend, partner or relative has to die within an in-patient facility.

We all know how susceptible relatives are to picking up senses of guilt and responsibility for issues that do not directly relate to themselves. I have no doubt that a significant number of carers would feel responsible for euthanasia having been performed, and I can only see grief being complicated further by carrying the burden of euthanasia.

As with the death of any young person, social structure and 'the right of passage' have been inverted such that elderly parents may be involved with or witness the death of their child. Add to this the knowledge of the source of their child's infection, for example drug use, or multiple sexual partnerships, and you will see how many parents are inevitably likely vicariously to take blame and be plagued by the question 'where did we go wrong?' The final sense of failure must be the cold and calculated decision to end the life of their loved one by euthanasia.

Implications for the Vulnerable

The vast majority of people with HIV-related disease are vulnerable because of society's prejudice - and here I would refer both to the drug user and the gay man. Secondly many are vulnerable because of financial pressure. Here again I would refer to the drug user but also to the young baby, perhaps born to a socially disadvantaged single mother. And thirdly some are mentally vulnerable, and in this I would refer particularly to those with neurological or intellectual problems complicating HIV. This subgroup I will look at in detail in one moment, but let us first look at the drug user and the baby.

Preliminary unpublished and rather loose statistics from New York suggest that in the last year of life drug users with HIV- related disease, particularly when it is neurologically based, spend 80% of their time in hospital or hospice. What, I wonder, will be the pressure upon the individual unable to leave hospital and increasingly disabled by HIV - will there genuinely have been an informed, independent and unpressurised decision by this person to end his or her life?

What about the woman infected with HIV who is pregnant and who wishes to continue to term? Well, we have already read in the medical press in the last six months of complaints by a number of young women in Lothian who have felt unduly pressurised to proceed with abortion rather than bear a child with something like a 50% chance of infection,- but equally, I would add, a 50% chance of being healthy. What will happen to the children who are born infected and who develop some problems with growth or neurological deficit? Who will decide when their quality of life fails to match up to social or economic yardsticks? We have absolutely no evidence that the quality or type of existence experienced by that child is so poor that the only course of action is euthanasia.

Care of the Intellectually Impaired
I now want to turn to the subject which I think is the most critical and important dimension that AIDS brings to euthanasia - namely, that of intellectual impairment (dementia or encephalopathy).

As I see it, there are three clear issues and again in a sense they come out of the same root - namely, the need that all of us have to feel in control of ourselves and our surroundings. I would say, of course, that this is entirely biblical if a person is moving under the authority of God (*cf* Genesis 1:28 on ruling the earth, and Galatians 5:22, 23 on the fruit of the Spirit).

What I am saying really is that I don't sneer at the anxiety that is generated for many people at the prospect of being out of control (that, of course, being a quite different thing from having the liberty and self-control to let go). The first major area that would fill many of us with foreboding, speaking personally, would be the progressive disintegration of mental faculties and personality such that our ability to communicate and relate gradually leaked away. Many of the people under our care are highly successful professionals who have achieved in their lives because of their intellectual ability. As John Greene, a psychologist at St Mary's with a very wide experience of HIV -related problems has often said, many of his patients would rather be dead than demented. I can empathise with that. As I understand it, the Dutch feel unable to bend the rules on murder and euthanasia to accommodate the termination of the life of someone who is in any way out of sound mind. This would seem, therefore, to exclude *de facto* the possibility of euthanasia in a demented person.

What then of the person who has assented whilst of sound mind to ask for euthanasia should they become demented? Two problems arise. First of all, what is to be judged as the point of intellectual deterioration or impairment that justifies the execution of euthanasia? Secondly, whose responsibility is it to judge that that time has come? Is it, for example, to be some objective intelligence quotient or the response to certain questions or is it to be a time when family feel unable to cope or relate to the patient? If it is the latter, then the brunt of responsibility will then fall on carers and clearly this is unacceptable.

Secondly, and I think this is a very important point, at a time when someone's intellectual faculties are blunted such that their communication is impaired, what evidence do we have that that person's emotional or spiritual state is the same as when they decided to opt prospectively for euthanasia? Can we be sure that they still wish euthanasia to take place?

Again, taking the subjective evidence of which we are all aware - that people have spiritual and emotional dealings at a time of semi–coma or altered awareness - it seems to me clear that the deepest roots of a person are still labile and open to change, independent of mental faculty - perhaps even more so now that their mind has been disengaged.

Would we therefore in the name of mercy (*i.e.* compassion - suffering with) consider it right to terminate a life simply on the evidence we had that a person's remaining life was of no value when, to the individual at that particular time, it had taken on a profundity of significance that they were unable to appreciate or even conceive at the time when they were of 'sound mind'? I cannot answer that question and I would challenge anyone else to try to.

With such uncertainty and imponderability I see no way in which euthanasia could be countenanced in this circumstance, and I think the potential for profound guilt and complicated grief in carers would be very high. I have purposefully not given weight to the argument that as a person's intellect and personality disintegrate, their insight and concern about their mental and physical state become obtunded, although this is of course a factor in whether or not they are happy or peaceful despite indices that may suggest otherwise.

My third major point relates now to the demented person as a vulnerable individual.

Without making a political jibe - in a climate of monetarism and economic stringency, the financial and social burden of a demented person is considerable. In the New York experience of people suffering with significant dementia, as I have said, about 80% of their time is spent as an in–patient. Do we seriously think that decision–making on the quality of life of a demented person would not in any way be influenced by financial constraints or the pressure on beds? Frankly, I doubt it. Are we sure that the difficulty in medical or clinical care of a person may not in some way influence our perception of their quality of life over against our quality of life in caring for them? Frankly, I doubt it. What, for example, of the single, chaotic, dementing drug user? How do we judge that person's quality of life given that their indices of quality may be at such variance with ours? I find the questions raised and the uncertainty around dementia to be such that I personally would find it impossible to make a balanced judgement in any such situation.

Finally, the probability of ending a life when that person still has an emotional and spiritual agenda may be sufficiently high that we are substituting our perception of an horrific death by dementia with the horror of an administered death when that person is not ready.

In Conclusion
God forbid that we should ever seek to fulfil the unmet needs for symptom control in the dying by introducing euthanasia for those who will never enjoy the benefits of adequate palliative medicine.

I read in the humanist press that the deprivation of people's freedom to die by euthanasia is the withdrawal of a fundamental human right. I am afraid that I have to look at the other side of this and say that were there any evidence or possibility that an individual's life would be cut short in error as a result of any legislation or guideline supporting euthanasia, I could not support that even outside the Christian framework, though this buttresses my understanding that the existence of government and legislation is for the protection of the disadvantaged, poor and vulnerable.

In concluding, I repeat that I feel that the opinions of people with AIDS differ from those with HIV infection alone. These are open to change and I have evidence to support that. There is an urgent need for widespread and excellent palliative medical services for all the population as a tangible symbol that euthanasia is not an option.

Finally, I will end as I began, by saying that the case against euthanasia does not rest upon sanctity of life, and yet I must quote the King's Mandate - the pinnacle of what God wants to do with and through us to establish his kingdom.

Our quest is for dignity, hope, freedom and healing for our patients as they pass through death.

'The Spirit of the Sovereign Lord is upon me, because the Lord has anointed me to preach good news to the poor. He has sent me to bind up the broken-hearted, to proclaim freedom for the captives and release from darkness for the prisoners, to proclaim the year of the Lord's favour and the day of vengeance (restitution) of our God, to comfort all who mourn, and provide for those who grieve in Zion - to bestow on them a crown of beauty instead of ashes, the oil of gladness instead of mourning, and a garment of praise instead of a spirit of despair. They will be called oaks of righteousness, a planting of the Lord for the display of his splendour' (Isaiah 61:1-3).

12

Euthanasia: The Hospice Alternative

Dame Cicely Saunders

Voluntary euthanasia has been put forward as a last freedom for a patient suffering from an incurable illness. When I became a doctor in order to develop new ways of caring for people dying with malignant disease, I knew nothing of that solution to the problem but simply aimed to give freedom from pain - total pain, a whole experience with its components of physical, emotional, social and spiritual distress. Since 1967, when St Christopher's opened as the first modern research and teaching hospice, it has aimed to encourage people to develop similar work in a variety of settings. This has happened - there are not only many independent hospices around the United Kingdom and now the world, but also Home Care Teams, Hospital Support Teams, Palliative or Continuing Care Units and a host of individuals, although a major hospice characteristic has been truly multi-disciplinary team working. The word 'hospice' has in fact changed from being only a noun, signifying bricks and mortar, into an adjective, denoting a recognizable set of skills and attitudes.

The whole hospice movement is still involved with a concern for freedom - freedom from inappropriate treatment, and freedom to use as fully as possible the last part of life without any open or implied pressure to end it prematurely. I would like here to approach two main areas. First, the present potentials in appropriate treatment for those with terminal illness and, secondly, the opportunities given by such treatment for growth and reconciliation at this time for these patients, their families and their friends.

We have seen great advances in appropriate treatments for terminal illness since the terms 'ordinary' and 'extraordinary means' were set out by Pope Pius XII in 1957, with the directive that the latter need not be employed. (Here I must point out that while I am a Christian and try to abide by Christian ethics as I understand them, I am not a Catholic and my paper stands more upon medical and social values as I believe these to be our common ground with those who advocate euthanasia.)

Let me turn first to potentials in treatment. A great deal has been learned about intensive therapy since I entered medicine to work in the field of pain control back in 1951, and there have been many illustrations quoted, often by the Voluntary Euthanasia Society, of the truth that we tend first to discover what we *can* do to rescue and prolong life and only later those occasions when it is right that we should do so. There are times when it is better for the patient that the medical team should desist.

Since the late 1960's we have all been learning a great deal about this, so that treatment limited to relief and support has now come to be widely recognized as a

challenging, rewarding and accepted part of medicine. For
example, 'palliative medicine' was recently recognised as a
speciality in which training should be available for Senior
Registrars in posts approved by the Joint Board for Higher
Medical Training. There is also a growing academic
interest in this field, and a spread of such interest and
teaching generally, with several journals and much other
writing available. Alongside, and in part at least due to
this development, has come a more widespread
recognition of the fact that a doctor's duty is not only to
aim to preserve life but also to relieve suffering and ease
the pains of dying. Decisions to limit treatment in this way
appear to me not to need recourse to the courts, as has
sometimes happened in other countries. This has been
well spelled out in the recent report of the British Medical
Association's Working Party on Euthanasia, who refer to
'non-treatment decisions' as being appropriate in certain
situations. I myself would have preferred the term 'limited
treatment' as suggested by Professor Brian Jennett of the
Department of Neurosurgery in Glasgow when he reported
in *The Lancet* on a recent international working conference
on this subject. I believe this emphasizes the all-
important truth that at no time should patients be deserted
by their doctors, but that all the skills of the multi-
disciplinary team may be needed to maintain relief and
support to him and his family to the end of his life. This will
still be treatment, and not a change to a soft option called
'care' or the medical washing of hands accompanied by the
remark 'there is nothing more that can be done'.

But, sadly, such decisions still fail to be made, even
where a patient makes his wishes known. I quote here
from Christian Barnard's book *Voluntary Euthanasia*. He
refers to a man of seventy-eight suffering from carcinoma
of the bowel and very severe emphysema. He said to his
doctor, 'You mustn't try to save my life. I am ready to die.
The machine is worn out, and the mechanic must now give
up.' 'No,' was the reply, 'this is not a hospital which allows

patients to die like that. We treat you here, we don't just let you die.' Unfortunately, what happened to that patient is all too familiar. After pointless surgery he developed problems with his lungs, and was intubated. During the night he somehow managed to disconnect the respirator. And in the bed there was a note, written in a shaky hand. The message read: 'Doctor, the real enemy is not death - the real enemy is inhumanity.'

There may well have been a fear of litigation, but there was no medical nor ethical reason why this man's request to be allowed to die should not have been met - by medical treatment of his obstruction and any other symptoms, to relieve the discomfort of his last days. That could and should have been done.

A suitable form of treatment in such a situation has been researched and documented in the general medical press by Dr Mary Baines and others from St Christopher's.[1] What was needed in this case was not a change of law but proper consideration of a patient's adequately informed consent, and skill to ease his passing.

This is a most important area for the spread of better public information. People do not always realize that no treatment, and that includes artificial feeding and hydration, should be carried out without their consent and that they need not resort to changing the law to establish this - it is true now. Where the patient is no longer competent, attempts should be made to discover his likely views from his family and consider carefully his quality of life. Here I must emphasize that dying people need less and less food, and the group we care for can almost always drink what they need. Thirst is better helped naturally than

---

[1] M. Baines, D.J. Oliver, R. L. Carter, *Medical Management of Intestinal Obstruction in Patients with Advanced Malignant Disease.* The Lancet, 1985, ii, 990-993.

by the discomfort of tubes, and unnecessary hydration often leads to extra distress.

Misunderstanding here has much potential for alarm, and this is illustrated in the BMA Report's comments on the society's National Opinion Poll, where a clear majority of those sampled voted 'yes' to the question 'The law should allow adults to receive medical help to an immediate peaceful death if suffering from incurable illness that is intolerable to them, provided that they have previously requested such help in writing.' Much turns on the one word 'immediate', and a clear opinion can hardly be derived on the basis of a single word which may well not be understood by a respondent trying to interpret a complex sentence. In the light of what I have already said, you will realize that the hospice position is that such a law should not be introduced and that there are better answers to the problem.

Like Professor Jennett and many others with experience in the field, I think that to use the term 'passive euthanasia' for decisions to limit treatment or to control symptoms at some risk of shortening life confuses this complex issue and can blur it dangerously. The BMA Report refers to that term in quotes and the whole tenor of their Report is to emphasize that such decisions have to be made as part of medical practice, with due regard for patient autonomy. Many now believe that such autonomy can be extended by using a form of 'advance directive' or 'living will'. The form suggested by the recent King's College Working Party does not ask the professionals concerned to take the step of deliberately hastening death, but does include a general directive that the person concerned does not wish to have certain specified forms of treatment in terminal illness but rather care and comfort - even if the measures taken may incidentally shorten life. They do not, and we believe cannot, direct that life should be taken actively.

This can, of course, only give general instructions but should be carefully regarded. A proxy, or someone with enduring power of attorney, may help in interpretation in the particular situation which may arise. For example, to pin a painful fractured neck of femur is not the same as heroic surgery, but both may be included under the same general directive. Further discussion is needed, as in this whole field. The Report is neither the first nor the last word on the whole subject of euthanasia. Today's conference is just such another word.

Advance directives would enlarge the area of choice for those who complete these forms, and I think this, too, is an area where we may have some agreement with others of differing views. Some hospice doctors have reservations, and they and many other doctors do not think a patient can use them to ask us to kill him. As the BMA points out, there are limits to autonomy - we cannot expect someone else to do what they judge to be wrong, let alone unlawful, at our behest. But once palliative treatment, good communications and family support are present, many such requests fade away. Yet, not all - and we must face every challenge of that kind with both personal and professional help, constantly learning more and developing our practice.

In talking of the personal potentials in terminal illness, I know I am speaking for other hospice doctors, many of whom I know as members of our Association.

Good communication is a condition for personal growth in terminal illness. Unless a patient can talk with his doctor, ask questions when he is ready to do so and receive (often gradually) careful and truthful answers, he will not be facing his real situation. Some people, even in a hospice, will continue to deny what is really happening. Most wish to talk, but there are no general rules here except that we must all listen. What we have been hearing have been mixed feelings and changes of mind, a sorting out of what is important, a look at personal values and a search for meaning. Those outside our field may be surprised to know how often we witness a journey from much anger, guilt and fear into acceptance, peace and a continual personal growth. Hospice is a place of discovery, and even those who seem too tired to make any progress at this stage can often be seen by those around them to make real achievements in the part of life that consists of 'being' rather than 'doing'. Of course, we are at times at our wits' end as to how to help, and have to sit listening with no answers to give and nothing but an attempt to understand. We do not belittle anyone's feeling, but we know from experience that the great majority will battle their way through and bring something truly creative even out of desperation. An honest facing of such negative feelings can be liberating.

But what of those who do not battle through? Those who feel defeated, and only long for the end? A few in hospices - more elsewhere? We believe they cannot direct others in law without putting silent pressure on the majority. As an elderly lady wrote to *The Times* some years ago: 'Human nature being what it is, euthanasia would not be voluntary for long.' A right to die could all too soon become a presumed duty to die. Dependent people are very vulnerable, and easily feel they are nothing but a burden. The few we cannot help by good care and personal concern, and who some feel need a law permitting euthanasia, would undermine the confidence of very many others. Surely it must be very hard to believe in continued interest and care, if a quick release has been offered - even if it has been refused? Better by far the assurance of care that continually aims to enhance the sense of personal worth - even at this stage - as part of the whole of a life's experience.

I am not saying that we *never* get sustained requests, but over many years we have found them to be rare - and I am speaking here for hospices generally. We do not think that a law should be introduced to meet these few anguished situations, for it would undermine the confidence in care of a far greater number who are asking us for help to relieve and share their suffering, and not asking us to end it by deliberately hastening death. And we are learning new ways of relief all the time.

Such hospice experience now concerns not just a few anecdotes, but many thousands of patients a year. I asked all medical directors if they agreed with the brief synopsis of my approach. I had a ready response, and all of the replies agreed with this position. We do not believe that we can work together with the Voluntary Euthanasia Society, or on the Netherlands pattern, although we recognize that they too have a concern for suffering people.

The potential for achievement is not limited to a patient on his own, but to him as part of a family network. Palliative hospice medicine is equally concerned with communication and support for the whole group. Where this is given, requests for a quick ending from those around the patient also fade away. A terminal illness in the family gives opportunity for much unravelling and reconciliation, for all the movement that can be facilitated by a crisis and which so often brings a new closeness in relationships. Over and over again we see people find confidence in their own capacity to meet this part of life together, and then to move through into the loneliness of bereavement. On many occasions they have needed all the time that the illness gives.

We are privileged in a hospice team, whether it is in a separate unit, in part of a hospital or out in the community, but we do not have the monopoly of such skills and attitudes. We have been able to focus, concentrate, research and teach and that has spread widely both in this country and overseas. But there are many others concerned with appropriate treatment, relief and support in all the other fields of medicine. Of course it has not spread far enough, but we must all tackle the complex clinical situations that are being met in an ageing population with positive answers and confidence in the potential of all the people we meet, not offer a quick exit from problems, however daunting they may appear.

Above all, we need to assert that people are inherently mysterious, with potentials they do not recognize in themselves until tested - though they may need encouragement to believe that their own inner core of personality continues to be recognized right through all vicissitudes.

To try to sum up, let me pick up on some of the comments from the many letters I had from hospice medical directors endorsing this position. We do *not* agree with the Voluntary Euthanasia Society when they say there is no difference between killing and letting die. That depends on the situation of the patient, whether we face an acute crisis in an otherwise heal ʾy person or care for an irreversible condition. The fact that there may be borderline cases does not invalidate the broad contrast between euthanasia (in the sense of deliberately hastening death) and alleviating treatment. We see so many patients who have been healed of a sense of worthlessness - and medical and nursing care, coupled with personal concern, can do this. They would never trust us for relief and support again if they had been advised that death was an immediate option. Years ago, one of our patients said to Lord Raglan about his bill in the House of Lords, 'You would give me a temptation I do not want to have to face.' We would present people with an intolerable dilemma when they need support to take courage and trust us never to think they are a burden. Those most experienced in meeting the difficult medical, nursing and, above all, personal and social problems that are now referred to hospice teams are the very people who see the most compelling arguments against euthanasia, understood as the deliberate shortening of life. We know something of the potentials in treatment - and are learning all the time - and we believe in personal growth, even to the end of life, however diminished it may look.